To Ma

Best

Ed Marshall

7-28-00

JUMP-STARTING AMERICA

JUMP-STARTING AMERICA

AMERICA

The Grass-Roots Revolution

EDWARD M. MARSHALL, M.D.

GRASS-ROOTS PRESS
A Division of Happy Hills Homes, Inc.
BRANSON, MISSOURI

Grass-Roots Press
P.O. Box 7609
Branson, Missouri 65615

Library of Congress Catalog Card Number: 94-096698
ISBN: 0-9643618-0-9

Marshall, Edward M.
    Jump-starting America: the grass-roots revolution

    Includes index.
    1. United States — Current affairs and social issues. 2. Grass-roots activism and volunteerism. 3. Education. 4. Crime and drugs. 5. Relationships. 6. Environment. 7. Health care

First Grass-Roots Press hardcover printing January 1995

10 9 8 7 6 5 4 3 2 1

Printed in the United States of America

To my family, the cornerstone of my life — especially my wife Linda, and our adult children Anna, Jeff and Alex. And, to all the great volunteers and activists of America who strive to bring their dreams into realities — whatever is good in America could not exist without you.

ACKNOWLEDGMENTS

Without Margaret Talcott's skillful help, I might still be trying to figure out how to organize ideas and stories into a book. Margaret, I thank you for getting me started.

Jeff Marshall, my older son, turned out to be my principal editor. He proved to be tough-minded, talented and very helpful. Best of all, he has a genius for entertainment, and had good suggestions for adding some spice to this project. The cartoons were his idea. Thank you, Jeff, for being there for me.

Speaking of cartoons, Roger Luteyn kindly supplied me with two original cartoons especially for this book, and I'm grateful to him for his good work.

My daughter, Anna Paul, besides being a designer of women's fashions, also helped design this book's jacket. I can't thank her enough for somehow finding the time to do that job, despite her very busy schedule.

Any reader of this book will know how strongly I believe that everyone needs a support group, or at least a support person. Besides thanking all of my immediate family, I want to express my appreciation to my cousin Diane August whose supportiveness represented a "beacon of light showing the way to completion" for this work. That light had to keep on shining for nearly four years.

Eli Blavin, a computer whiz in addition to being a fine gentleman to work with, was responsible for getting the manuscript

ACKNOWLEDGMENTS

ready for the printer. Thank you, Eli, for your expertise and hard work.

I gratefully acknowledge the following authors, cartoonists and their media representatives for their permission to reprint: Dori Previn, John Wooden, Dana Summers (Washington Post Writers Group), Jeff Stahler (NEA, Inc.), John Trever, Ed Stein, Mike Smith (North America Syndicate), Eric and Bill Teitelbaum (Tribune Media Services), and Scott Stantis.

The news media, including radio, television, newspapers and periodicals, clued me in about many grass-roots stories going on around the country. I'm grateful to *The Los Angeles Times, The New York Times, The Wall Street Journal, Investor's Business Daily, USA Today* and others too numerous to keep track of. That gratitude extends to all of the reporters, and to all of the activists and volunteers without whom there would be no stories to tell.

Finally, I want to thank former Secretary of State George Shultz for corresponding with me and for allowing me to reproduce his letter in this book.

CONTENTS

PART I
GETTING INVOLVED IN
THE GRASS-ROOTS REVOLUTION

CONTENTS

PART II
BIG ISSUES CALL FOR
BIG ANSWERS, ACTIONS AND RESULTS

CONTENTS

PART III
REWARDS AND DECISIONS IN OUR HANDS

PREFACE
Dreams That Work Wonders

We have to dream first. That's how it all starts. Otherwise we don't know what we're working toward. And our dreams do work wonders. They move us to act, to transform those dreams into realities.

We dream of a day when every community has schools that really work. Schools that our children actually like to attend. Schools where parents send their children with confidence that they will be safe and will return home bettered by each day's experience. We dream of a day when schools, assisted by parents, teach their students by the age of 18 everything they need to know to be useful and productive citizens. Citizens who have readily employable skills, or who are ready to go on to higher education for careers that require extended education and training. We dream of schools that accomplish all of these things, and even help teach human values. And all at a price

xiii

families can afford.

We dream of a day when all the individuals and groups of every community live in harmony. We dream of communities with very low crime rates, where murder is rare and even shocking. Communities where people respect themselves and others, where group pride and group identification never replace personal identification and personal responsibility. Communities where people respect their own ethnic identities and appreciate those of others, accepting diversity with grace. Where people can be comfortable living, working and playing among people of every group and type, so long as all come in peace.

We dream of communities where people can count on themselves and on each other, where help is never far away. Communities that organize to make themselves safe and healthy, that run their own affordable and effective health care systems. Communities where people work together to find the best among them to elect as representatives and leaders.

We dream of communities where individuals and families thrive, where love is shared. Where people abuse neither themselves nor others. Where joy is the common experience, and suffering and grief are limited to the irreducible amount that life requires of us.

Carl Sandberg said, "Nothing happens unless first a dream."

Dreaming of what we want requires us to act or be left unfulfilled. Acknowledging our dreams makes us responsible for them. Some choose to deny that they have dreams in order to evade that responsibility, to avoid having to act upon them. But satisfaction and joy are reserved for those who acknowledge their dreams and take action to realize them.

When we're in action to fulfill our dreams we feel truly alive. Even the process of fulfilling them makes life joyful and worthwhile. Imagine seeing our dreams actually come true! And we can never run out of more dreams of betterment for ourselves and others. Not before we run out of days.

The trick is to get into action and never stop. Can you picture Thomas Edison stopping short of his ten thousandth try that created the electric light bulb? Can you imagine Martin Luther King giving up on his civil rights goals?   I dream of a day when no one in any

In dreams begins responsibility.

— W. B. YEATS

Dreams are the touchstones of our characters.

— HENRY DAVID THOREAU

community would consider being uninvolved in the fulfillment of their dreams. Not having the time to satisfy our dreams is not having the time to be alive.

By the time you read this book, with its many stories of people getting involved and making a difference, more progress may have been made toward solving America's "Big Issues". The Big Issues of today are the ones we dream of turning into the Big Successes of tomorrow: education, crime and drugs, health care, personal environment and relationships. New people, maybe even you and I, will be among those creating new success stories. For some of America's issues, there are still too few stories to tell. What's most important is that the stories told here, and the examples of grass-roots solutions given, inspire us to keep our dreams alive, and to do what it takes to bring them into reality. We are America's jump-starters. We can make it happen.

INTRODUCTION

Writing a book isn't an easy job. It's not something I would do lightly, nor would I advise anyone else to. What happened to me is that I became inspired. I knew I'd find no peace until this book was written.

Like everyone else, I've noticed the continual worsening in recent years of America's "Big Issues" — problems of education, crime and drugs, health care, personal environment and relationships. And like almost everyone, I'd been good at complaining about all of our problems and lamenting, "Why don't THEY do something about it?" That was B.I. (Before Inspiration).

On my road to becoming inspired, certain realizations began to overtake me, just as they may have overtaken you in recent years.

REALIZATION #1: "THEY" never have and never will solve America's problems.

Most Americans for decades have believed that the "powers that be" both inside and outside of government would solve our problems. If only we would elect the right politicians, or the better political party... If only we had new laws and new programs, even at the cost of massive spending, taxes and public debt...

1

INTRODUCTION

Well, we've tried both parties, several times each. Many elected and appointed officials have been sincere and imbued with the highest motives. They meant well. They still mean well. We've seen all sorts of laws passed and new programs tried. We've watched politicians and their promises come and go, we've paid burdensome taxes, we've wished and we've waited. "THEY" have not only failed to solve our problems, the problems have grown much worse.

REALIZATION #2: Finally, with one awakening glance in a mirror, we realize that WE are the "THEY" for whom we've been searching and waiting.

Gradually over the decades, and massively in the past few years, millions of Americans have involved themselves in community-betterment activities of all kinds. Gallup Poll surveys in the early 1990's show almost 100 million Americans, about half the adult population, spending over 4 hours a week doing volunteer work. Our level of involvement has nearly doubled since 1977.

No longer do we think of "activists" as wild-eyed political fanatics, and "volunteers" as people who do things for free because they're retired or no one will hire them. Today we ARE activists and volunteers. We tutor students and assist teachers while pushing for local school reforms. We recycle and join the huge crowds who clean long stretches of beach in a single day. We help fill and place sandbags when floods threaten. All over this country we Americans are reclaiming a sense of neighborhood and community spirit as we get involved to make a difference.

REALIZATION #3: WE, at the grass roots, CAN solve America's Big Issues of crime and drugs, health care, education, our environment and relationships.

We've seen grass-roots volunteers (people without powerful positions or wealth) put independent candidates on the ballot in all states, provide the impetus for environmental legislation to be passed, press corporations to become better citizens, cause local school reforms to occur, and literally provide the arms and legs that

2

allow our hospitals to function. With nearly 100 million Americans involved, it's no longer farfetched to say that WE can solve our largest problems, the ones that THEY obviously can't.

REALIZATION #4: America's Big Issues won't be solved until more of our volunteer projects become innovative enough to transform the personal and social frameworks in which problems occur.

Even with all the wonderful millions of activists and volunteers doing good work, the Big Issues problems aren't being solved. In fact, they still appear to be getting worse overall.

Most of today's grass-roots volunteer work, while important and praiseworthy, amounts to a futile attempt to apply more and more *Band-Aids* to rapidly expanding wounds. We provide remedial tutoring for school dropouts, we help the homeless, we assist victims of crime and parolees. But we don't do nearly as much to prevent dropouts, broken homes and the social problems that contribute to crime, drug abuse and homelessness. Most of our efforts are reparative, not innovative, transformational or effectively preventive.

However, my research did find that an explosion of innovative grass-roots activism packing a transformational wallop IS beginning to stop the slide in education. And I discovered increasing examples of partnerships between government and grass-roots organizations that are getting results, such as the "Adopt-A-Highway" programs, and corporate sponsored scholarships combined with internships at state-run universities.

Yes, I began to be inspired by what is already happening and by what can be done when we volunteers get behind innovations that transform issues rather than just repair damage. "Teach for America" and Education Alternatives, Inc. are examples of educational innovations. And groups providing clean needle exchanges, and those mentoring inner-city youths are examples of innovations needed to transform our crime, drug and health issues. While many of our grass-roots innovations are inspiring and on the right track, they are clearly still not enough to resolve any of the Big Issues we face.

3

INTRODUCTION

But, this inspiration, combined with my realizations, became the driving force that pushed me into action. It became clear to me that, if I really wanted to experience fulfillment, I had two jobs to do.

My first job was to get directly involved as a volunteer, helping out with support groups at transitional housing facilities for the homeless. I liked it. I still do. Whatever I give never seems to match the satisfaction, and even joy, that I receive there. I found that it isn't easy to distinguish the giver from the receiver in volunteer work.

Then, the second job I had to do in order to be fulfilled — more of an activist's role — became clear:

Someone needed to point out that America has gone through three eras of dealing with social problems. Originally we depended almost solely on self-reliance and neighborly help to solve problems. Then we became a society almost totally dependent on government activism. And now we are reverting to enormous grass-roots activism and volunteerism, sometimes coupled with government participation.

Someone needed to point out the immense power of this recent surge in grass-roots activism that is revolutionary in scope.

Someone needed to provide information about people and programs that are helping, and about existing systems that are useless or even harmful.

Someone needed to give specific examples of innovative programs capable of largely solving each of America's Big Issues.

And someone needed to do all of this in one book.

"Someone" had a big job to do. And since I was already inspired by my dreams of community betterment, the time had come for me to act. Part of my inspiration was realizing that we can only do things NOW, and we can only do them HERE. Looking into the mirror,

INTRODUCTION

seeing the reflection of my real life, I knew I had to give it my best shot. I knew that waiting and hoping that THEY will do something is not the way to have better, stronger and healthier individuals, families and communities. Getting into action and never quitting until dreams are brought into reality, and THEN not quitting because there are other dreams waiting to be realized, is the only way to fulfill our lives, to be fully alive.

So what else could I do? I wrote.

PART I

GETTING INVOLVED
IN THE GRASS-ROOTS REVOLUTION

1

YOU AND I <u>ARE</u> AMERICA:

The Power of Responsibility

When we hear knocking on America's door, only we can answer. It's either us, or there's nobody home. You and I clearly are America — as individuals and as members of families, groups, communities and the larger society. America lives, does and is, only as all of us live, do and are. Our whole society is no better or worse than its individual members.

So we have the responsibility that goes with being members of the American society. We either take that responsibility or we don't. The consequences follow accordingly.

When things are going wrong some people say, "Hey! Don't look at ME!" Not getting involved keeps some people's comfort zones intact. Temporarily. The price is having nothing to say about the outcome. The price is being and feeling powerless. All that's left is empty, useless complaining. And the problems get worse. Sooner or later everyone's comfort zone is disrupted.

But there are those who say, "Please tell me what I can do to help". Or, "Here, let me give you a hand." These people access the power to make a difference just by their willingness to get involved.

Many of us don't realize how powerful we are until we're caught up in a crisis that gets us into action.

Our power to be who we want to be, to have the families, relationships and communities we desire, all comes from us asserting our responsibility. This power is available to all of us on a daily basis. We get feelings of accomplishment and joy when we use it.

HOW DO WE "ASSERT" OUR RESPONSIBILITY?

The first step is being willing to ACKNOWLEDGE that certain things are true: (1) We CARE about an issue; (2) we're INVOLVED with the issue because we care; (3) once we care and are involved, it's only natural and quite easy to identify our DESIRED RESULT; (4) realizing that so many things, though difficult, are possible, we acknowledge that the desired result is POSSIBLE to attain, though we may not yet know how.

"Asserting" something calls for action. So the second step requires our willingness to be COMMITTED to making our desired result into a reality. Commitment reflects the strength and passion of our desire to get a result. It's what makes us willing to get into action.

And that's the third and final step — to BEGIN TAKING ACTION here and now, no matter how small our first act. To make our effort pay off, we'll have to STAY in action until the result is achieved. This is a necessity if we are to be true to ourselves.

Whether our first action involves networking to find others who will work with us, writing a letter, or doing anything else is less important than that we are NOW in action.

If you've ever followed the acknowledgment, commitment and action steps, consciously or automatically, congratulations! You asserted your responsibility. Which made you powerful. How powerful? You probably got the result you wanted if you were persistent.

WHO IS INCLUDED IN THE "GRASS-ROOTS REVOLUTION"?

The simplest definition of the grass roots is "ordinary people".

The implication is that there are people who are not ordinary. Not-ordinary-people are those in positions of authority and power, whether government officials or the "powerful elite" of society because of wealth or position.

But this simple distinction between the "grass roots" and the "powerful elite" breaks down under scrutiny. When ordinary people accomplish extraordinary results in their families and communities, they look pretty special, don't they? Kind of elite, even. And when powerful and wealthy people fall from their lofty heights after being exposed by wrenching scandals, they look pretty ordinary, don't they?

It gets fuzzier. When ex-Notre Dame basketball coach Digger Phelps helps build decent housing for the inner-city poor, or when former President Jimmy Carter picks up his hammer and does the same, alongside dozens of volunteers, are they the elite or the ordinary grass roots? I think we're all ordinary people capable of doing extraordinary things.

So if all of us can be part of grass-roots action, let's try another definition: The "grass roots" include everyone engaged in community-betterment activities when not acting in an official capacity, and when not compensated by money.

"Grass roots" can also describe ALL people who are not officials — even those who aren't using their power by asserting their responsibility.

This definition bothers me a lot. There isn't much point in referring to people as members of the grass roots if they aren't doing anything. Or at least not doing anything to better their communities or fulfill their own lives. Maybe that's why our newer dictionaries recognize "grass-roots" as an adjective, so that we can describe real people doing real things. You know, "grass-roots activists" or "grass-roots volunteers".

You know how strong the roots of grass are. They survive winters, droughts and weeds. It's just that some grass roots are less vigorous than others. Let's face it — some are totally dormant year-round. I hope more and more at the grass roots activate themselves before the weeds...well, you get my drift. You and I can get ourselves, and influence others, to be more powerful.

11

WHAT'S THE DIFFERENCE BETWEEN AN "ACTIVIST" AND A "VOLUNTEER"?

All activists are volunteers, but not all volunteers are activists.

Most volunteers are helpers. They carry out the daily tasks and functions vital to the success of any grass-roots program. Volunteers expect, and get, no monetary compensation. They do what they do because they love doing it. They believe they are doing good work for their communities. Their volunteer efforts fulfill them and give them some measure of joy.

Most volunteers don't organize grass-roots programs, or take the ultimate responsibility for planning the steps required to make the efforts successful. Activists do both. Then all volunteers, including activists, work to get the results. Activists are the grass-roots entrepreneurs and top management (I'm not referring to the paid staff hired by large activist groups). As with businesses, successful grass-roots efforts require good people and good work at all levels.

Compared to the raucous variety common in the 60's and 70's, today's activism is more broadly based and diversified, quieter and increasingly effective. Some strident activism is still around. Noisy, disturbing demonstrations appeal to those who believe their cause will otherwise languish. Nearly all grass-roots activists and volunteers work to better their communities using only peaceful methods to achieve their goals. Only a few, substituting desperation for commitment, cross the line into violent behavior.

AMERICA'S MAIN ISSUES THAT NEED OUR POWER

Five main issues need our helping power NOW: education, health care, crime and drugs, our personal environment and our relationships. Each issue affects the others, and making improvements in one makes all the others better.

For several decades, most Americans have taken it on faith that THEY (government and school officials, religious leaders, therapists — anyone but us) would make all these problems better. It hasn't happened. No matter how well-intentioned or funded, government clearly cannot solve all of our personal, family and community problems. Not even close.

As a result, cynicism has surfaced. As has resignation. But something else has surfaced. People aren't waiting anymore. In the past few years involvement by grass-roots activists and volunteers has soared. Today nearly 100 million Americans average over 4 hours per week helping better their communities.

Parents, teachers, business people, members of the clergy and students are already reforming education. Volunteers at home and in the workplace are taking recycling to new heights. Pressed by activist-led groups, businesses are doing a better environmental job.

But America's massive grass-roots revolution has only begun to get behind the innovative solutions needed to prevent or greatly improve our five major problems. This is especially true with regard to crime and drugs, health care and relationships. Most activism and volunteerism is still limited to cleaning up the damage and caring for the victims of unsolved problems. These valuable and heroic *"Band-Aid* brigades" need to turn more of their efforts to truly transformational and preventive work.

WHAT WE REALLY CAN MAKE HAPPEN

It's as though we've been waiting for someone to stand up and say, "It's okay. Go ahead. You don't have to keep waiting and hoping that THEY will take care of these issues. You've waited long enough. Now just get in there, get to work and be a part of the solution of every issue you care about. You can do it. I have confidence in you."

There. It's been said. Now it's okay for you and me to solve the problems of education and our personal environment — even the issues of crime and drugs, health care and relationships. We can make any and every kind of community-betterment happen, provided we don't wait for anyone or anything. All we have to do is get started and never stop until we have the results we want.

It all goes back to the fact that WE ARE America. We have the power that comes from acknowledging and acting upon our responsibility. You and I can set goals, make plans, organize, take steps and accomplish. I intend to enjoy it. I bet you will, too. Let's go!

*Make voyages! — Attempt them! —
There's nothing else...*

— TENNESSEE WILLIAMS

2

PEOPLE ARE MAKING A DIFFERENCE:
So Why Are Problems Growing?

T he evidence is overwhelming — people, in unprecedented numbers, <u>are</u> making a difference all over America. Yet, paradoxically, huge, widespread problems persist and some are even getting worse.

CREDIT WHERE CREDIT IS DUE

Don't get me wrong. Some things are getting better because of the grass-roots revolution.

People volunteer one at a time. That's what some 100 million Americans have done. Each of them had to be courageously committed to get involved. It's important to acknowledge — to recognize — ourselves and others for accomplishments as volunteers for community-betterment. When we acknowledge ourselves or others, we feel good, we grow, we glow, and we achieve unity with what and who we acknowledge.

Hundreds of volunteers of diverse ethnic backgrounds, led by actor and community activist Edward James Olmos helped clean up some of the mess of the 1992 Los Angeles rioting. Thousands of volunteers nationwide have taken part in massive clean-ups of beaches, neighborhoods, urban graffiti and parks. "Adopt-A-Highway" programs have become a great example of public-private partnerships for community-betterment. Almost every sizable business has a recycling program, often operated on a volunteer basis by employees. Aluminum cans, for example, are being recycled at a rate close to 75%. Twenty years ago the rate was below 10%.

Thousands of volunteers across America are involved in tutoring and mentoring programs. More than ever, people are volunteering time in hospitals and hospices, delivering food to the needy via community food banks or directly to shelters and "rescue missions", and delivering prepared meals to the elderly and disabled (Meals on Wheels, for example). Volunteers have organized shareholder groups to help make better corporate citizens, while other groups boost conservation of water, forests, wetlands and wildlife.

Individuals and groups beyond counting are also boycotting, donating, raising funds, writing, speaking and performing to boost their favorite community-betterment causes. It's important that we recognize and acknowledge this great work, and yet —

MORE "INNOVATIVE" GRASS-ROOTS ACTIVISM IS A MUST

With all the billions spent on social programs by government, the additional billions donated to charitable organizations, and with vast millions of Americans involved as volunteers, our Big Issues problems persist and some are still getting worse: crime and drugs with deteriorating neighborhoods, worsening relationships among individuals and groups, and a health care crisis for millions of Americans. How can this be?

I took a look at — an overview of — the kinds of volunteer work being done, and I found a simple explanation. What's missing is the innovative and transformational grass-roots activism needed to jump-start America out of our Big Issues quagmire. What's needed are specific innovative plans that are really capable of solving major problems if enough of us actively support those plans.

Volunteer work falls into two general categories. Both are very important, and the activities of some groups overlap the two categories. The "reparative" category has been most prevalent over the years, while the "innovative and transformational" category is beginning to emerge.

When I describe a grass-roots program as innovative, I'm referring to the program's ability to transform, to produce a new set of conditions and circumstances that enhances the lives of people and communities so that problems that need reparative work tend not to occur. Innovative activism is both life-enhancing and problem-preventing.

Examples of reparative volunteers include those who work with the Red Cross and other voluntary relief organizations after disaster strikes. These groups assist the victims by providing shelter, food and clothing. Blood is donated, collected and distributed.

Reparative work is done more to provide relief than prevention. Arguably many of these activities do also prevent problems, not just repair them, and some reparative efforts bring transformational results. Sometimes it's the volunteer whose life is transformed by the experience of being of service to others.

America's marvelous volunteers greatly improve the lot of the thousands they serve. And it is crucial to note that most natural disasters and many illnesses are not preventable with our current level of knowledge and technology. So America needs every person willing to serve their community as reparative workers, and I intend to continue my volunteer efforts in this category.

Yet, and it bears repeating, with all the reparative work accomplished with billions of government tax and borrowed dollars, plus billions more of private charity and with millions of committed and involved volunteers across America, our problems persist and grow. Neither a lack of funds, nor insufficient numbers of volunteers, explains America's unsolved and growing problems. That's right. More money and more volunteers, alone, will not turn around the growth of our problems.

What we need are specific grass-roots programs and strategies that are of such quality and scope, so right-on-target that real transformation will occur. It's a main purpose of this book to

17

describe a few such winning strategies that all of us can get behind. I'm talking about grass-roots activism that is really capable of solving Big Issues.

Some of the examples I'll describe are already up and running, and just need to be refined and expanded. Others are in the proposal or planning stages, and haven't been tested. I also give some of my own specific examples of the kinds of innovative work that are likely to pay off, to give us the results — the community-betterment we all want and seek.

SPECIFIC INNOVATIONS

Innovative grass-roots activism is finally growing in America, particularly in education (Chapter 7). Parents, business people, educators and clergymen have joined forces to add values to the curriculum, to provide local control and choices of schools. Some states, responding to pushing from the grass roots, are trying charter schools. Whittle Communications has a project to re-invent the American school on a private basis that public schools could emulate.

Privatization of public schools may well be the direction of the future, and community-based non-governmental schools is the specific type of privatization I favor. Already several public school boards have contracted with universities and private companies to help run their schools.

We can argue that while these grass-roots efforts in education are in the innovative/transformational category, they are also reparative. After all, students who are in the middle of a mediocre educational experience are to be uplifted into one or another new and improved educational experience. The counter-argument is that the old inadequate system is not being fixed or improved, it is being replaced or transformed. NEW SYSTEMS of education are being invented. We're not just fixing one student, one classroom or one school at a time.

No matter what educational innovations are tried, simultaneous improvement in the other Big Issues will be needed to get worthwhile results. No Big Issue problem exists in a vacuum.

18

It is better to be making the news than taking it...

— WINSTON CHURCHILL

Although education is the issue with the most rapid growth of grass-roots innovation as of this writing, we have already seen an impact on the environment, and to a lesser extent, on crime and drugs, health care and relationships.

Chapter 8 calls for a new system of regulated drug access for confirmed addicts, and other innovative measures that can only come to pass with a big push from the grass roots. One result from this successful grass-roots campaign will be a huge reduction in crime based on the need of addicts to obtain money to support their illegal habits. The system proposed stops far short of full legalization, and would replace our badly failed and enormously expensive "War on Drugs".

Chapter 9 describes a new system of health care, involving community-based non-governmental control that would provide true health care democracy. The result will be higher quality and more efficiently delivered care, markedly lower costs and equally greater accessibility. I call it the Community Health Association, and its health care plan is "CHAP", the Community Health Association Plan.

Chapter 10 proposes personalizing the environment by starting with our own mind, body, home and workplace. And all of the Big Issues are interwoven: keeping our homes free of toxic materials and our bodies free of harmful chemicals we might inject, swallow or inhale are both personal environmental issues and health issues. Success in these areas adds to our self-esteem, improving our self-relationship. Living in a nearly crime-free neighborhood provides safer schools, and enhances our social environment and our health.

The "Warm Line" is presented as an innovative grass-roots plan to help assure well-being in everyone's personal environment, to help prevent the need for "Hot Line" and "9-1-1" calls. "Warm Line" volunteers will contact neighbors often enough to help those whose personal, home or neighborhood environment becomes threatening or dangerous. It's time we move beyond our presently prevailing system of responding as concerned members of the community only after personal or family tragedies occur.

Community and neighborhood "support groups" (Chapter 11) already exist in various forms in some cities. Such groups need to become a grass-roots activity in every community to help people have the best possible relationships with themselves (self-esteem, for example), and with others. Failed family relationships are a major cause of unhappiness, substance abuse and juvenile delinquency. That's why helping build better relationships deserves to be the highest ranking Big Issue for grass-roots activists.

THE BIG ISSUES, AND THEIR SOLUTIONS, ARE INTERWOVEN

The tie-ins between issues are impressive and important. For example, health care and the environment are often, mistakenly, treated as distinctly separate issues. We often see the inter-relatedness of all the Big Issues, as when broken marital relationships result from, or lead to drug abuse and crime. Then homelessness and ill health can follow, with the children of the broken families doing poorly in school or dropping out. The order in which these interlocking miserable events occur varies. But by being aware of how totally interwoven the Big Issues are, we are better able to plan and effectively operate innovative grass-roots solutions.

My specific proposals for innovative grass-roots activism are intended to transform America's Big Issues within a few years. Other grass-roots interventions may be as good or better. You may have your own plan in mind. The bottom line is for all of us to increase our involvement in innovative grass-roots strategies now, to get the results we want as soon as possible.

America's Big Issues are challenging. Almost overwhelming. The good news is that effective solutions that we can carry out are available, just waiting for our involvement. Every important movement and trend in American history, starting with the revolution by colonists, has come from the bottom up, never from the top down. As this is written in 1994, most volunteer work being done by Americans remains confined to the reparative category. Imagine the results we'll enjoy when we've increased our innovative and transformational grass-roots efforts!

3

THINK BIG, START SMALL:
Choosing Issues and Getting Started

To this point we've established that: you and I **ARE** America; asserting our responsibility gives us the power to make a difference; millions of people are already involved doing exactly that; more activism of the innovative type is needed to resolve, reduce, or even stop the growth of America's most serious problems.

A gap exists between what can be accomplished at the grass roots, and what is actually happening. How can you and I help close that gap?

You see, I'm Thinking Big. I want major results for us, for our communities, for America over the next few years. We at the grass roots are fully capable of jump-starting America. It's my commitment to contribute to that process. My way of measuring the success of this book will be our progress in resolving the Big Issues, not the number of books sold.

But I've Started Small — asserting my responsibility in small ways. First I started leading sessions of support groups for people living in transitional housing programs in Los Angeles and San Diego, as a volunteer, of course. I began doing some recycling. Then I became a "Big Brother". All of these activities were small steps, but I was now in action.

And I was still Thinking Big. Could I put together a book that would encourage more of the creative, innovative type of grass-roots activism? Would such a book help lead to faster and better results? Could the book help start a computerized networking system for activist volunteers?

So I Started Small. I managed to get a literary agent. Sort of. And I started to write. Lots of false starts over a two-year stretch. I still needed to earn a living for myself and family, so the writing took longer than planned. But then I found myself with a manuscript, two fine editors, but finally no agent and no publisher. Now I had to plan to somehow publish the book myself.

Lots of small, one-at-a-time steps, with lots of detours, road-blocks and disappointments along the way, accompanied by hard work. Just like real life, it occurs to me. And all worthwhile when the results fulfill our dreams.

Sure I was committed, determined not to quit no matter what. But, like everyone else, I needed support. And, like everyone who aspires to accomplish something more than the ordinary, I got plenty of negative support. Here's a sample: "You're not a well-known personality, so we don't want your ideas." Negative support and other obstacles just make doing it — going all the way and getting the results — that much sweeter in the end. Along the way, I've had the support of a few precious people. It doesn't take many, but everyone needs at least a tiny support group, or even one support person.

I kept thinking big and doing small steps. I don't plan to ever stop using this system. It works. The thing to remember is that you can only fail by defeating yourself, by stopping yourself, by quitting, by not taking the next step. I'm dumbfounded to realize how many years it took me to really get this message.

What has all this got to do with YOU? That's entirely up to you. If you're ready, all that remains is to choose the issue or issues that mean the most to you, think big about the results you want to see achieved, then start small in that direction and never stop until you have those results.

Once you choose your issue(s) and get started, it will be an

A journey of a thousand miles must begin with a single step.

— LAO-TZU

exciting journey.

Why think big? There's no other way to end up with big accomplishments. Why start small? The biggest project can only be accomplished one step at a time.

Choosing issues will usually mean choosing just one issue, or at least, just one issue at a time. Trying to handle too many issues at once can be just as overwhelming as trying to handle too many steps at once.

Sometimes very personal reasons, perhaps involving a tragedy, will determine a person's main issue. One example: After their son Adam disappeared, John and Reve Walsh started the Adam Walsh Resource Center to help find missing children.

Perhaps you already know what your most important issue is. Is it something that's touched your life? If you don't immediately know which issue to work on first, look at your own life and your surroundings. Weigh your concerns, hopes and dreams. Would you like to work on one of the "Big Issues" this book deals with — education, health care, crime and drugs, our personal environment, or our relationships?

After choosing your issue, decide how much time you want to spend working on it. Do you have two hours a week, or more, that you can spend without jeopardizing your relationships, your job or other important commitments? Almost everyone can find that much time. The big surprise comes when people find that they enjoy their volunteer efforts so much, they want to spend more time on them.

Okay. You've chosen your first issue and you know what your time limitations are. You're being realistic and starting small (still thinking BIG). What exactly are you going to do? You need a direction in order to plan and carry out your first step.

Do you know of an organization that shares your goals regarding your issue? If so, you can contact the organization, plan to attend a meeting, or find out if there's a committee you can join that's working on exactly what you hope to accomplish.

Suppose you've checked the phone book; you've been to the public library to check the *National Directory of Non-Profit Organizations, Charitable Organizations of the United States* and other directories; you have networked with your family, friends and co-workers; and you've even networked with Project Jump-Start as explained in the "AFTERWORD". Suppose after all your searching you haven't found a suitable existing group, committee or organization that shares your goals regarding your issue. At this point you can either start your own group or you can tackle another issue that already has organized support.

Chapter 12 deals with the nitty-gritty of organizing a committee, group or organization to accomplish your goals. Meanwhile, you're sure to experience satisfaction just by choosing an issue and taking a first small step that's in line with your Thinking Big about the results you want.

4

WHY US, WHY NOW:
We Can Help a Little or Be Hurt a Lot

Yes, there is satisfaction, joy and fulfillment to be gained by our grass-roots efforts. This is especially true when we start to get the results we're after. But, along the way —

Even if you're not religious, or even if you're an atheist, at some point you'll run into enough obstacles as you work to accomplish your goals as a grass-roots activist or volunteer, that you'll ask, "God, why me?"

I won't presume to be answering for God, but there are some compelling reasons for you and me to be actively involved in community-betterment, and to be involved now.

AMERICA'S BIG UNSOLVED PROBLEMS

America continues to have inherent strengths and greatness: our freedoms, the diversity of our people, and our generally strong free enterprise economy. But America clearly needs the innovative grass-roots help of millions of its citizens now.

Over the years government has spent trillions on education,

crime and drugs, health care, the environment and, yes, on poverty, the final common pathway when failure occurs in any or all of the other issues, and especially when relationships also fail. The main result of all this spending is that we've built a vastly intrusive and expensive bureaucracy matched by troublesome and huge taxes, budget deficits and national debt; and we've built a class of nearly helpless and dependent welfare recipients.

Now is the time for the government role as would-be universal problem solver to be largely replaced by innovative grass-roots activism. Our grass-roots revolution continues to grow and show its power to get results. It's clear that only after much more community-betterment results are achieved by grass-roots activism will government's role diminish. For better or worse, the burden of proof is on us ordinary citizens to prove that WE can accomplish far more than "THEY" ever will.

Today we see a trend in government toward contracting out and privatization, including some private management of prisons and public schools, increasing use of out-of-court mediation and arbitration, and several private overnight mailing systems. Increasing numbers of government/private sector partnerships are being used successfully, including transitional housing programs, the Big Brothers and Big Sisters organizations, and Meals on Wheels. We see neighborhood watches, civilian patrols and Guardian Angels helping to combat crime, many of these in full cooperation with local police. We see a wide variety of volunteer mentoring and teaching programs at our neediest schools.

These innovations are happening for a reason. It has become painfully clear that government alone cannot solve every personal, family and community problem. Our country's problems have become severe enough to give large numbers of us Americans a sense of urgency to get involved, "or else".

Washington, DC's homicide rate is higher than any other "civilized" COUNTRY's homicide rate. There is increasing pressure to build new prisons due to overcrowding that is leading to early releases for dangerous, violent criminals. Tens of thousands of school children carry guns and other weapons to school every day, and use them all too often. Some school dropout rates are falling, but forty

percent, and higher, dropout rates are still common in inner-city schools. Divorce rates and broken homes are rampant. The figures for unwed teenage mothers, abortions and sexually transmitted diseases, already high, continue to climb. The AIDS epidemic is a growing menace, spread mainly by casual sex and dirty needles. 37 million Americans have no health insurance, and many more have limited access to quality care. And while American medical technology is topnotch, the everyday delivery of care is marred by unnecessary, expensive and dangerous treatments and testing, and is too often devoid of common sense and good judgment.

So we need to get involved "or else" what? Most of us don't want to wait to see how bad things can get.

WHAT OUR INVOLVEMENT CAN MEAN

We've given ourselves the mirror test. One honest look tells us that WE are the "THEY" we've been waiting for to make things better. Experience has shown that persistent efforts, consisting of innumerable small steps by people acting voluntarily alone or in groups of all sizes, do bring significant beneficial results.

Okay, it has to be us. And we have a pretty good idea of how grim things can get, so we realize that we ought to get into action soon. But why "here and now"?

We can't do anything yesterday, and tomorrow is only a prediction. And, we can only do things HERE, exactly wherever we may be. As the late comedian "Lonesome" George Gobel used to say, "Always remember: Wherever you go...there you are."

But most of us have to earn a living. And no matter how dedicated we are to community-betterment and to being part of the solutions, there's a lot more to life that most of us want to continue to enjoy. Just how much work, how many hours a week are each of us going to need to devote to innovative grass-roots activism in order to make a significant difference?

Here's some good news. No, make that "GREAT" news! Except for a few people, the activist leaders who will need to be more involved, most of us will never need to spend more than a few hours a week to make a significant difference. Of course there will be

32

those who WANT to spend a lot more time than that. Some retired folks spend as much time on volunteer work as anyone would on a full-time job.

How can I be so sure that just a few hours a week will make such a difference? I have two kinds of evidence. The first is that many of us, perhaps including you, have already been making a difference when spending that amount of time. The second kind of evidence is mathematical. If tens of millions of people are enthusiastically involved a few hours a week, the results are bound to be spectacular if the activities are innovative, well organized and on target.

More good news. It's important that any successful grass-roots effort be sustained over time. So it's good to know that very few people, involved just a few hours a week and seeing the results they want clearly becoming reality, are going to suffer burnout. People who aren't being overburdened don't walk away from their own joy and fulfillment.

THE PRICE OF NOT GETTING INVOLVED

On the surface, not getting involved looks like a viable, even inviting alternative. That's before we take a deeper look at what the consequences will be for us.

The argument in favor of "not getting involved" goes something like this: "Let's save ourselves hours of effort. Why take part in cleaning the beach when we can just leave our garbage lying around and enjoy a swim? Who needs to avoid dangerous chemicals, drugs and overeating? Sickness only hits OTHER people. And why worry about the school system? We pay our taxes, don't we? And crime? Just build more prisons, hire more police, spend more money until it's fixed, right? Hey, aren't we winning the War on Drugs? THEY are taking care of it all for us."

You and I know better. There really is a price of not getting involved. We don't get the America, the communities or the relationships we really want. We don't have the satisfaction of being part of the process of bringing community-betterment into reality. So we don't get the reality or the satisfaction.

*We haven't the time
to take our time.*

— EUGENE IONESCO

All we get by not being involved is what comes at us, like it or not. We give up our say. We give up our power. We end up <u>feeling</u> powerless, and we're left to grumble and complain that THEY should be making things better.

If WE don't make a difference "here and now", we'll find ourselves just trying to survive in a decaying society. Isn't that exactly what millions of Americans are doing today in our larger cities?

WHAT'S IN IT FOR US?

Suppose we do it. Suppose we assert our responsibility. Won't it be a lot of work? Yes. And won't there be difficulties, obstacles, stumbling blocks, disappointments and setbacks? They're guaranteed. There's no pay, right?

There's no salary, but there's lots of payoffs.

To me, the biggest reward we get by getting involved to make a difference is the opportunity to experience the joy and fulfillment that comes from volunteer community service. If you've ever been involved in being of service to other people on a volunteer basis, you know the feeling. You've discovered that you cannot give more of yourself than you get by giving. In a sense, you grow and glow in the process.

There's also the joy of being involved in a project you choose, playing a role you select to help get the results that you decide you're committed to getting. Then, yes, you will face plenty of obstacles along the way, but your chosen commitment and sense of accomplishment will sustain you.

Let's not forget the results. The successes and accomplishments you produce will be very sweet rewards (Part III delves further into the likely far-reaching effects of grass-roots activism). You're bound to feel rewarded and pleased when you see community issues solved and you know you were part of the solution. Even if some of the results you sought are not obtained, you'll have the satisfaction of knowing you gave your best effort.

Best of all, you ultimately get to have more of the America you really want, the kind of community and relationships you want. In fact, by being willing to acknowledge and assert your responsibility, you get to be your true self, the person you're capable of being, living the life you fully and freely choose.

God doesn't require us to succeed; he only requires that you try.

— MOTHER TERESA

5

GRASS ROOTS
ARE GROWING:
Can We Reach
"Critical Mass"?

Not everyone, and especially not all of today's younger people, are familiar with the term "critical mass". I'm not referring to a crucial religious ceremony. Those of us who grew up under the specter of the world's first nuclear explosions know that critical mass is the amount of plutonium required to generate the chain reaction that leads to a nuclear explosion.

Is it possible to reach a critical mass of grass-roots involvement, so that when a certain level of activity bearing on a particular problem is reached, that problem will be quickly minimized or even eliminated? And if such is possible, are we currently approaching that critical mass with regard to America's major problems?

Why do I ask? Two reasons: (1) It would certainly be encouraging if the answers are "yes"; (2) most of our Big Issue problems are still worsening in the face of massive grass-roots involvement.

It's hard to believe that we need many more than the current number (some 100 million) of active volunteers. The negative view is that worsening problems in the face of such large-scale involvement proves that no amount of grass-roots activism will resolve our

39

Big Issues. In this view, grass-roots critical mass can never be reached, and only Draconian governmental intervention has any chance to succeed.

The positive view is that what's at stake is not the number of volunteers, but rather, the type of activities that they're engaged in. This view holds that if even a small percentage of today's grass-roots activists and volunteers get behind good innovative solutions, critical mass can be reached and the Big Issues will be largely resolved.

We know that the scope of grass-roots activity in America has been expanding. Today there is organized fund-raising for virtually every category of disease by specialized volunteer organizations. Twenty years ago there were only a handful of disease-specific organizations. The number of environmental groups has also mushroomed, impacting our lives considerably. Volunteers on school campuses have increased by the tens of thousands, and groups exist to combat or alleviate virtually every conceivable problem.

But are the problems growing faster than the organizations and their ability to solve those problems? Does growing grass-roots activity only represent a futile attempt to apply more and more *Band-Aids* to rapidly expanding wounds?

The answers may be both "yes" and "no", depending on the issue.

If we divide the results of grass-roots activism according to time, for example before the 1990's and after 1990, it's probably fair to say that until the 1990's grass-roots activism was almost entirely reparative (except in the environmental arena). So it's not surprising that problems have been growing faster than repairs can be made. With the advent of innovative and transformational activism, which has yet to hit anything close to its full stride, we're seeing the beginnings of a turnaround in education, and perhaps with regard to the environment. The next few years will show us whether or not large-scale and lasting betterment of education and the environment will occur. It absolutely will in education if present trends continue (see Chapter 7).

We not only need to make a distinction with regard to the results of activism before and after 1990, we need to consider the fact that innovative grass-roots activity is in its infancy with regard to crime and drugs, health care and relationships. And there's no question that the rate of wound expansion is outpacing the *Band-Aids* with regard to these issues.

If America's grass-roots activism can be influenced to focus on transformational and innovative solutions to the still-growing problems of the "Big Issues", then I have no doubt we will reach the necessary critical mass. But except for education and possibly environmental issues, I'm equally convinced that we're NOT yet approaching critical mass regarding the other Big Issues of crime and drugs, health care and relationships. I'm committed to being part of the process that must and will come from grass-roots transformational activities with regard to every one of the Big Issues.

We've already witnessed the complete turnaround of some of our most troubled schools and students, brought about by innovative principals, teachers, community leaders, activist parents, private companies and wonderfully responsive students. Some of my favorite stories along these lines are in Chapter 7.

Even if our grass-roots efforts don't produce a critical mass effect, those efforts can still be very important and helpful. Big Issues would just take longer to be largely resolved without a critical mass kind of phenomenon.

But we do have evidence that a critical mass type of rapid improvement may occur. We know that when education improves, earning power increases. When poverty is eliminated, family relationships often improve, and people with good education, who are well paid and are enjoying good family relationships are most likely to take good care of themselves and make proper use of professional health care. Such people are less likely to be susceptible to major substance abuse or a life of crime. This interrelatedness, or interweaving, of the Big Issues is likely to help produce the kind of rapid, snowball-rolling-downhill effect that I'm referring to when I talk about achieving fast results by reaching "critical mass".

Clearly, progress on any issue enhances progress on all the others. We know this interrelatedness exists because we've also seen its downside as America's Big Issues problems have worsened. (You might say we've been approaching "Critical MESS".) The interrelatedness has worked like this: People with poor education tend to stay poor, often get involved in drugs and crime, have less satisfying relationships, tend to take less good care of their health and have less access to health care. The issues can be taken in any order — children with lack of parenting at home, or who have been abused, often grow up unable to relate well to others, may become child abusers or get into trouble with substance abuse, remain poor, take poor care of themselves, and so on.

So we have plenty of evidence that improvement in any one area will make obtaining improvement in the other areas much easier. This is the stuff that critical mass is made of. This interrelatedness offers us hope for much faster results than we could possibly get otherwise from our volunteer efforts. And those efforts will need to emphasize implementing high quality, innovative and transformational solutions if we are to succeed.

PART II

BIG ISSUES CALL FOR BIG ANSWERS, ACTIONS AND RESULTS

6

WHERE NEW DIRECTIONS ARE MOST REQUIRED:
Targeting "Big Issues"

I hope you've emerged from Part I with your battery charged. Maybe you were already fired up and active as a grass-roots volunteer. Either way, we all want to be sure that our energies are being expended in directions that will give us the results we want, as quickly as possible.

This doesn't mean we can't have some patience — as long as patience doesn't become complacency, procrastination or settling for very small results.

If you believe as I do that most of the Big Issues continue to show deterioration — manifested by broken families and poor relationships between individuals and groups, rising crime and drug abuse rates, poor accessibility and affordability of good quality medical care — then you'll probably also agree that new directions are needed for grass-roots activism in these areas. Even in education and the environment, Big Issues that may actually be showing net progress from grass-roots involvement, there is a long way to go and innovative directions in these areas need to be identified and acted upon.

If we can find the right innovations — ones that are capable of transforming the conditions that lead to big problems — we'll then be able to avoid and prevent those problems at their source. The idea is not merely to do battle with the Big Issues. We need to transcend and outstrip them so that, over time, the Big Issues problems are no longer big at all.

Not every innovation is going to work. Some will have to be modified or replaced. Others will work well, but not as fast as we'd like them to.

And we know from experience that we can't transform the conditions that cause our major problems by means of today's grassroots reparative efforts, as important as that work is. So how will we maintain reparative volunteer services and still implement the new transformational services we need? I can think of two ways: (1) New volunteers will join in, doing only (or mainly) innovative work; (2) many who are already involved will spend more time implementing innovative plans, and less time as reparative volunteers.

IDENTIFYING THE BIG ISSUES

You may wonder why I haven't included poverty, whether inner-city or rural, as a Big Issue. Or what about racism, inter-group hatred and discrimination based on age, gender, sexual orientation, nationality or religion? I see poverty as the result of failures among the Big Issues already named. And relationships, as we will see in Chapter 11, includes relations between races and all groups.

I don't intend to minimize other issues that can be tackled successfully by the grass roots. Reforms are needed in our legal system, which too often fails to be a system of justice. The grass roots could also play a major role in reforming politics in America so that we have fewer lifetime, professional politicians in office. I would like to see the full privatization of welfare and all so-called entitlements. Non-governmental and non-profit community organizations controlled by the citizenry and run largely by volunteers, would handle these matters. The result would be immense savings of tax and debt dollars, and better service to recipients with more meaningful help than government agencies can provide.

But this book, and particularly this section (Part II), deals with specific innovative solutions to the five Big Issues I believe are the most important and fundamental ones for America in the 1990's and into the next century: Education, Crime and Drugs, Health Care, Personal Environment and Relationships.

TALK OF CHANGE PROVOKES OUR INSECURITIES

Whenever I call for sweeping changes to transform education or any of the other Big Issues, I notice how scared to death many people are of change. It's as though the certainty of even hell-on-earth is preferable to the uncertainty that comes with trying something new.

Here are some clues that you're dealing with people scared silly by any new ideas for change: You're describing your proposal to an adult who regresses to thumb-sucking as you speak; or, as you tell people your plan, they cringe with a pained or fearful look on their faces; the most obvious case, less frequently seen, is the person who reacts to the threat of trying something new by saying, "I want my mommy."

Okay, I'm exaggerating. But only a little. So, why do people react this way? I see all of us humans as being fundamentally insecure, although our insecurity doesn't always show. It makes sense. We're aware (after our teenage years) of our vulnerability and mortality, and we're sensitive creatures. We have our normal fears: fear of death, fear of rejection, fear of conditions getting worse.

We know change could worsen things, so change is often seen as a threat, which causes the fear that makes us feel insecure. That's why opposition to anything new is almost automatic. Something new has to be sold. Fear has to be overcome. Sales people and advertisers face this challenge every day. I'm dealing with that challenge in this book, too, as a salesman of new grass-roots solutions to Big Issues problems.

On the plus side, if it weren't for fear, courage wouldn't exist. It's courage that allows us to go on despite our fears. Our fears are real. They make us insecure, but we don't have to let them run our lives.

Then, what can we do? We need to reassure ourselves that any changes wrought by the grass roots can be cast asunder by the grass roots. This ought to free us up to look at the possible good that something new can bring.

There was tremendous fear when the automobile threatened to replace the horse and buggy, but many people felt better by keeping their horses and buggies for a time after buying their first car. A large percentage of American colonists feared the revolution and remained Tories even after the British admitted defeat. For some, opposition simply meant loyalty to the King, but plenty of others were fearful that independence wouldn't work out. Fortunately, only a few people in each generation need to have the courage to overcome their insecurity in order to make good changes happen. It is these courageous few who become activists for change.

THE OLD DIRECTIONS THAT DON'T SOLVE PROBLEMS

We know that governmental and grass-roots *Band-Aids* such as welfare and remedial education can only hope to slow decay, or possibly hold the line. These efforts don't solve the Big Issues.

THEY don't eliminate problems. The government's War on Drugs is doing no better than Prohibition did, and is actually making our crime and drug problem WORSE. Our public school system, with some exceptions, continues to function poorly. Medicare, Medicaid and city/county hospitals haven't cured the ills of our health care system. Even in the private sector, high quality and thoughtful health care is too expensive and is often simply not available at any price, despite the presence of insurance coverage and first class technology. Whether the issue is education, crime and drugs, or health care — creating vast bureaucracies and spending huge sums of tax and debt dollars have turned out to be worse than futile.

THE BIG ISSUES ARE INTERRELATED

No human problem stands alone. Let one problem develop, and others will follow. Prevent or eliminate one, and others will not occur or will begin to improve. This is the opportunity and the challenge for all of us at the grass roots.

*He knows nothing;
and he thinks
he knows everything.
That points clearly
to a political career.*

— GEORGE BERNARD SHAW

When all children, including inner-city youth, attend dynamic, exciting and challenging schools that deal with real life and lead to real careers; when all people have full access to quality health care; and when people enjoy good relationships within their families, households, neighborhoods and communities — there and then you will find disappearing poverty, discrimination and intolerance, as well as diminishing drug abuse, crime and illness. So what are the needed innovative grass-roots plans that will accomplish these results?

Part II takes on the Big Issues one at a time from the grass-roots perspective. Innovative systems that grass-roots activists and volunteers can implement are presented. We'll see that a few of the innovations are already in operation or on the way, and some successes can be claimed. Others are just in the planning stages, and some of these innovations are either partly or totally my own. They will only become solutions if I succeed in giving them away, so that they become YOUR innovations and YOUR plans. When many of us work together, we're able to make good grass-roots plans into community realities. Otherwise, no matter how promising any proposals appear to be, they remain unfulfilled dreams.

The results we want will begin to be achieved when you and I show up, committed and ready for action.

7

REAL SCHOOLS AND REAL EDUCATION:
A Promising Future

Of all the "Big Issues" America faces in the 90's and beyond, education is likely to show the most improvement over the next ten years, based on what's already happening. And, yes, it's about time! From school boards, principals and teachers to students, parents, the clergy, businesses and concerned citizens, the intensity of today's efforts at the grass roots to improve American education reflects widespread concern for our current system's failings.

Until the last few years, we Americans expected that "THEY", which you now know means the government or anyone other than you and me, would do something about schooling problems. Perhaps more money or different elected officials would help. Taxes were raised, many bond issues were passed, and new people were elected. Spending per student skyrocketed. But, starting in the mid-1960's, things just kept getting worse for American education. Some of us stood by, resigned and apathetic, while others complained.

More recently, WE have been getting busy. Community activism has mushroomed and innovative reforms are being planned and implemented. I can't fully predict which modes of change will pre-

Government is like a big baby — an alimentary canal with a big appetite at one end and no responsibility at the other.

— RONALD REAGAN

dominate, or how long various improvements will take. But, the downward slide IS halting and major improvement appears to be around the corner, or at least down the road.

WE volunteers and activists, by the tens of thousands, are taking responsibility, doing the job of improving education in America, and reaping the joys of making a difference. The activity is nationwide, and thousands more will surely be involved each year, based on the statistical trend. There is considerable data to suggest that a turnaround in education has already begun, at least in several locales.

Besides the many groups already in action reshaping and improving the way our children are educated, other innovations are still on the drawing board. This chapter presents the inspiring stories of individual teachers, principals and others who are achieving excellent results (and finally gaining well-deserved recognition). We'll look at some of their methods, some possible educational systems of the future, and ways all of us can help make American education better in our own hometowns.

THE PRESENT GRIM REALITIES

Hopes and dreams for the future aside, the present grim realities regarding our schools are the driving force behind today's growing grass-roots activism to improve education.

Today dropouts, violence, robberies, thefts, substance abuse and vandalism dominate too many of our campuses. Inner city drop-out rates often exceed 40%, even reaching 70%. Teenage pregnancy alone accounts for some 20% of all dropouts.

A statewide survey of school violence in Florida showed that 46,000 criminal offenses, ranging from murder, rape and robbery to simple threats of assault, were committed on state campuses in 1990. The Center to Prevent Handgun Violence reported that 71 people, including 65 students, were killed by gunfire on U.S. campuses from 1986 to 1990, and the numbers are probably worse since then. Like me, you've probably seen too many of those sickening newscasts showing children who have been shot and killed in school or on the way to or from school. Everywhere teachers complain that teaching

Reprinted by permission of SCOTT STANTIS

suffers under today's campus combat conditions. According to one estimate, some 90,000 schoolchildren carry guns to class every day!

Companies are spending millions annually to train employees WITH high school diplomas, and even college degrees, in the essential math and writing skills needed to do their jobs. If you're an employer, have you not marveled at how some of your employees could have spent so many years in school and come away with so little?

Scholastic achievement test results nationwide, particularly in math and science, have been dropping — confirming our educational deficiencies. Many believe that poor educational results are seriously undermining America's ability to compete in today's world marketplace.

Financial considerations in the 1990's don't make the picture any brighter. Everywhere tax-supported school systems are short of money, as administrative costs are high and recent recession tax receipts have been low. As state universities are closing some departments and reducing teaching personnel in others, students are having an increasingly tough time getting classes. Tuitions are up, and many school programs are threatened with elimination. Pouring more money into the system hasn't helped so far, and how much more taxes can you and I be expected to pay?

Families and communities are in turmoil. With the recent recession, students have been moved frequently from one school to another; divorces and separations add to that toll. In single-parent households, or two-parent households in which both parents work, parents are less available to encourage homework to get done, or to volunteer to help out at school. And besides the high incidence of crime and drug-use on and near campuses, the same problems beset students in too many of their homes.

It has become clear that, all too often, when innovative solutions to educational problems are proposed, or even legislated, the entrenched educational establishment often fights them to their extinction. How can useful change occur?

Given these grim realities of today, how can I predict a bright future for American education within the next ten years and beyond? You'll see.

PRESENT GREAT REALITIES

By far not all the current news about education in America is bad news. Much of the news is very good — and very inspiring.

Recognizing Great Teachers and Principals — Increasingly, the stories of truly great individual teachers and principals are being told. During the decades when we expected that "THEY" would take care of education, these front-line heroes at the grass roots were little recognized. Now that WE are getting involved, we're helping to give some of our educational heroes their long overdue recognition. We now see how important these miracle workers are to the education of our children and to our country. We also recognize that we need to learn how to train, inspire and reward many more of them.

I'll bet most of you, like me, remember one or two outstanding teachers who really got our attention, taught us well, even made a difference in our lives. Now grass-roots organizations, TV programs and even movies are telling some of their stories. The film *Stand and Deliver* presents teacher Jaime Escalante, who converted Latino high school dropout candidates into math whizzes. The 1989 movie *Lean on Me* shows how one principal's leadership motivated students and teachers to overcome adversity: how Paterson, New Jersey, principal Joe Clark expelled 300 "hoodlums" and brought unity and academic excellence to his troubled Eastside High School.

At an inner-city school in Brooklyn, where thirty students were murdered in four years, Principal Carol Beck instituted student-run mediation, diverted troublemakers out of the school and started new educational and guidance programs. In short, she stabilized the school to the extent that 80% of 1991's graduates went on to college. For her good work, Principal Beck received the American Hero in Education Award from *Reader's Digest* and the National Association of Secondary School Principals.

In Alhambra, California, high school science teacher Duane Nichols inspires 75 students to attend his special biomedical research studies class at 7 a.m. three times a week. Many of his students have exhibited at scientific meetings and have won awards and scholar-

56

ships. Alumni, inspired by Nichols to go on to medical and other scientific careers, write to thank him. Nichols says, "That is your pay, knowing you helped these kids...And I think I'm lucky. I work with kids who are vitally interested in what's going on around them, and they respond easily." He admits he pushes his students "to do the little extra." The willingness and ability of teachers "to push" our kids is obviously crucial.

Paul Cain, a teacher of computer mathematics at Ysleta High School in an impoverished Latino area of El Paso, Texas, achieved an unprecedented result: In 1992, five of his graduating seniors were accepted to MIT. Said Cain of his students, after crediting parental support, "You can't help but fall in love with them and wish the best for them. They are winners. When they wake up in the morning, they are winners." I believe that teacher Cain is also a winner, one who knows how to create winners.

In Inglewood, a low-income minority community in Los Angeles, two elementary school principals, Marjorie Thompson and Nancy Ichinaga, have led their students to achieve academic scores higher than those obtained in most schools in affluent areas. Both focus on reading and writing in the earliest grades, and find that they're able to transmit high expectations to teachers, parents and students. Each of these principals consider themselves the "principal teacher" at their schools. They encourage teachers to watch and learn from each other, rather than spend the same time attending district-sponsored workshops.

The common thread among all these outstanding principals and teachers is their profound love and care for their students, and their will and ability "to push" them. These qualities inspire both the teaching and the learning that take place.

A 1991 study on school reform by Brookings Institution senior fellow John Chubb and Stanford University Professor Terry Moe concluded that principals are crucial to improving education in America. That's not hard to believe. So, one challenge for us at the grass roots is to back the improvement of methods for training, selecting and rewarding outstanding principals.

New Types of Schools Involve the Community — New types of schools are being tried, including museum-based schools emphasizing science to elementary school children. In Los Angeles, one of these schools is to be operated as a joint venture between the school district, a museum and a neighboring university. More common are "magnet schools" that give students and parents a chance to choose a school specializing in a particular area, such as the arts, or technology, or aimed at particular groups of students, such as the gifted.

USC sponsors, and funds, a "Pre-College Enrichment Program" for inner-city youth. Each year, sixty minority seventh-graders, all average students, are selected for a six-year program aimed at producing university scholars. Full four-year scholarships are offered to all participants who meet admission requirements by the end of the program. After school and on Saturdays, the students gather on the USC campus for tutoring, and for lessons on ethics, public speaking, time management and decision-making. The process is also intended to boost the self-esteem of these students. Parental involvement is mandatory in the program's Family Development Institute. The payoff is clear: Early results show a 40% increase in A's and B's, as well as an immeasurable increase in the children's feelings of self-worth.

To encourage parents to further the education of their disadvantaged children, a Los Angeles program called EXXCEL (Educational Excellence for Children with Environmental Limitations) provides new, low-cost apartments for parents with school-age children in a low-income minority area. Parents get even greater breaks in rent if their children do well in school, and A's and B's will net a child cash, movie tickets or trips to Disneyland.

This fascinating EXXCEL program is the brainchild of developer-owners Kent Salveson and Dan Hunter. It's a cooperative venture with USC and local public schools. Even government agencies are involved, giving tax breaks and low-interest financing to the developers for providing low income housing. Some of the apartments will be occupied, rent free, by USC doctoral students in education, family counseling or psychology who will provide on-site family counseling and tutoring. USC has donated scholarships for resident children who ultimately meet minimum college entrance requirements.

The 46-unit structure that has already been completed in south Los Angeles could serve as a model for similar developments around the country. Plans for operating the complex include a drop-in station for police officers on patrol, a branch library open to the community — and a study room stocked with textbooks, computers and reference materials, and staffed by tutors and parent volunteers.

Parent participation is mandatory, and local elementary schools are also involved. Salveson is hiring part-time instructional aides from a local school to increase coordination between school and home, to help with tutoring and to monitor the tenant students' progress. Further good news: with all the apartments rented, the deserving developers expect to turn a profit and plan to build at least three more similar complexes.

(Having lived mostly in Southern California, I'm more aware of innovations there, but the specific grass-roots programs I'm telling you about in this chapter are meant to serve as metaphors for those occurring all across America, and as inspiration for others yet to come.)

We need to recognize that these new types of schools and incentive programs are based on the voluntary efforts of teachers, school and university officials, business entrepreneurs, parents and others. These endeavors don't appear in anyone's job description. Are you impressed that such diverse individuals and groups are able to work together to accomplish so much? I am! I'm also impressed by the obviously powerful commitment that drives them to do it.

Volunteers On and Off Campus — Besides the marvelous contributions being made today by outstanding teachers and principals, and by innovative schools and educational partnerships, individual volunteers have become increasingly involved in bettering education. In recent years there has been rapid growth of volunteer on-campus activity by parents and others in the community.

And many parents today are spending more time at home assisting their children with their studies and homework. One affluent school district spent over $10,000 to install a telephone call-in system so that parents can call and hear a recorded summary of what their child's teacher taught that day, what homework was assigned and suggestions as to what they should ask their children about that evening.

A less expensive system is now being widely used throughout Maryland. The program, called Teachers Involve Parents in Schoolwork, was developed by Joyce Epstein, co-director of the Center on Families, Communities, Schools and Children's Learning at Johns Hopkins University in Baltimore. In this program, every homework assignment involves parent participation: The students are required to talk to someone at home about the assignment or what happened at school that day.

Regardless of whether parents know what their child's homework is on any given night, whether they are unable or unwilling to help with it directly, parents can instill values and set high standards for their children, making learning a high priority. Lillian Brinkley, president of the National Association of Elementary School Principals, and a principal herself, suggests that if the parent doesn't understand the child's schoolwork, "let him (the child) be the teacher." Children love the chance to teach their parents, and parents who honestly tell a child they don't know something, and who are willing to be good listeners, are playing an important role, Brinkley advises.

Volunteers have also been filling holes left in the wake of budget cuts, doing everything from teaching art to running libraries and cleaning school grounds. About half of California's 1,048 school districts now have organized volunteer programs, and the number grows monthly. Kay Bergdahl, president of the California School Volunteer Partnership Program, a private non-profit group that organizes volunteer programs says, "I can hardly keep up with all the demand for (volunteer) workshops." Although parents make up the largest segment of volunteers, grandparents, business people and professionals, retirees and even high school students are helping out in growing numbers.

80-year-old Kay Woollett, and other residents of her Long Beach retirement home, have spent four hours every Wednesday helping nearby elementary schoolchildren learn how to read. For most of these students, English is a second language that's not spoken at home.

James Sanchez, a 34-year-old computer engineer, has been

mentoring a high school junior who wants to go to medical school but lacks the needed background and confidence to get admitted.

Where school districts once rebuffed volunteers, today most top administrators, principals and teachers welcome all the community help they can get.

The Los Angeles Unified School District had just 60 people volunteering their services in 1963, but by 1991 that number had grown to about 30,000! The San Diego Unified School District saw its number of volunteers grow from 5,800 in 1989 to over 12,000 in just two years. Even districts without formal volunteer programs report rising numbers of community volunteers assisting at neighborhood schools.

We know from data compiled by the National Association of Partners in Education based in Alexandria, Virginia, that there are over 2.5 million volunteers nationwide who provide more than a billion dollars in goods and services to school districts annually in recent years.

Specific Types of Innovative Reform — All over America today, spurred by grass-roots efforts, educational reform is taking two basic directions: LOCAL CONTROL, also known as "school-based management," and CHOICE, referring to giving parents choices of schools. While these two modes of reform have already proved useful, they don't go far enough. Critics, like me, point out that local control and even unlimited choices won't help much unless teaching methods and curricula are improved. So two more needed elements of reform are: RELEVANT CURRICULA and EFFECTIVE TEACHING, both of which are starting to receive more attention from grass-roots groups.

I'm adding ACCELERATED EDUCATION to the list, not just as another reform, but as part of my proposed transformation of our educational system and the lives of our teenagers and young adults. But since it's only on the drawing boards, we'll discuss this proposal further in the next section I call "FUTURE REALITIES".

Who are the people involved in the grass-roots groups pressing for innovative reforms? Parents, as one might expect, are very much involved in education reform groups, but businesses and business leaders (some are parents, too, of course) are taking an active, sometimes controlling role. Today corporate money supports innovative schools and scholarships. Businesses are increasingly forming partnerships with university-based researchers, and several corporations are paying the administrative expenses of some reform groups, including the costs of public opinion surveys and public relations efforts to help promote reform.

And when it comes to efforts to gain more effective teaching, even students are finding ways to help improve aspects of the educational process. One example: with the encouragement of San Diego sixth-grade teacher Rick Morris, his students wrote a book, *School Our Way*, which tells teachers some of the best methods that really work for classroom teaching. Way to go, kids!

Teachers' Unions and School Officials — Teachers' unions play a large role in advocating and opposing various innovative reforms. Most teachers' unions oppose parental choice, because whether choices are based on vouchers or otherwise, choice threatens public school funding and, of course, teachers' job security and pay scale. On the other hand, teachers and their unions frequently support local control, but are often reluctant to share that local power with parents and parent groups.

Trustees, school board members and administrators of public schools often side with teachers' unions in opposing reforms, especially when choice is to be implemented by voucher systems. Voucher funds go directly to parents, so it's easy to see why public school officials feel as threatened as the unions do. Clearly, this resistance is self-serving in a myopic way.

But there's also an associated arrogant belief, held even by officials of some of our most troubled school systems, that parents are incapable of choosing schools for their children, and that somehow attending "public schools" (a euphemism for government schools) is, **a priori**, a valuable and irreplaceable experience. Do you suppose they're referring to the experiencing of crime on campus, the barbed wire fences, the high dropout rates, or the falling scholastic achievement test scores? Perhaps it's all of these.

But most resistance to reform by school officials is largely to protect their jobs and authority. A few officials strongly opposing reform have even misused their positions and authority to embezzle public funds, as has been reported in Kentucky.

Not all school boards and teachers' unions are working to block reforms, to maintain their power and to hang on to a failing status quo. Many school boards are taking an activist role, and some unions have begun serious efforts to reduce administrative costs of education.

One specific reform strongly backed by teachers' unions is the slashing of administrative costs by reducing middle management, freezing administrative hiring and paying top administrators the same salaries as teachers. While these stands may deserve community support, they appear to reflect the unions' concern over "whose ox is gored" in the current atmosphere of school budget crunches.

Merit pay for teachers has been advocated by elected officials and community activists alike, but is generally opposed by teachers' unions. Superb teachers are often the objects of jealousy, as Jaime Escalante of *Stand and Deliver* fame found out. His local union may have engineered his re-election defeat as chairman of his high school's math department. Feeling unwelcome despite his incredible successes as a teacher at LA's Garfield High, Escalante resigned. Unions likewise resist giving up the tenure that protects the jobs of the most incompetent — the very teachers who parents, students, principals and school administrators all wish would get into some other line of work.

When it comes to changing teaching methods and curricula, teachers' unions seem to agree with the notion that beyond reform, a whole new American school is needed, one where teaching focuses on students becoming problem-solvers, and not just regurgitators of facts. This is an area of activism in which teachers and their unions have the opportunity to contribute mightily to bettering our educational results.

Teachers, teachers' unions, school administrators and officials will find that there will always be room for the best of them in American educational systems of the future, even if those systems no longer include the failed and discredited public schools that are being innovatively replaced despite all resistance.

Local Control Has Local Activist Support — In several communities parents, teachers and administrators have joined forces, forming local groups to combat bureaucratic roadblocks to reform. Such groups have succeeded in getting schools restructured — combining 6th, 7th and 8th graders into "Middle Schools" while moving 9th graders up to high school, thus replacing the old "Junior High" of 8th and 9th graders. The community groups have also fought successfully for innovative awards, special-interest clubs, electives and humanities courses in their local schools. The results of these reforms, clearly instituted only as a result of grass-roots efforts, include better school attendance, higher academic performance and improved behavior among adolescents.

Other issues that local activist groups have successfully addressed include obtaining local control to deal with school overcrowding, as well as more local control of budgets, curriculum and staffing — core issues in the "school-based management" reform movement.

In Los Angeles, LEARN (Los Angeles Educational Alliance for Restructuring Now) was formed by a small group of attorneys and business executives together with the Industrial Areas Foundation, a collection of neighborhood activists working for school reform. The group has raised over $1.5 million from such businesses as Arco, Southern California Edison and First Interstate Bank. LEARN, chaired by Robert Wycoff, chief operating officer of Arco (Atlantic Richfield Corp.), has organized task forces that include parents, community activists, UTLA (the large union - United Teachers of Los Angeles), school district administrators, and business executives. The goal of the program, accomplished in 1993, was to come up with a plan for more local control, giving each school's principal, teachers and parents more power over school finances, curricula, hiring and firing. Legislation could be required in order for the Los Angeles Unified School District and the state's Department of Education to give up that power. And the teacher's union, although fully included in LEARN, remains wary of the entire reform process.

Two other Los Angeles business-led groups — The Los Angeles Educational Partnership (LAEP), which funds classroom innovations, and the 2000 Partnership, formed to help the City of Los Angeles plan for the future — joined LEARN in commissioning a Louis

Harris poll. The poll revealed that 81% of the general public thought education money could be spent more effectively, and 90% of teachers agreed. Even 77% of school administrators thought funds could be better spent. 95% of parents said schools would improve if parents could make more decisions on campus! You don't often find 95% of people agreeing on anything. I consider this a powerful indicator that parents are ready for communitization (the ultimate form of local control) of public schools, which we'll discuss later in this chapter.

Parental Choice Takes Various Forms — In a sense, all "local control" proponents are competing with groups working for "choice," although both reform methods can coexist. Voucher plans, the most publicized of "choice" proposals, let parents choose schools — including private schools — for their children, and use tax dollars to subsidize the cost. Public school administrators and teachers' unions fear that parents will choose private schools, draining funds from public schools.

The Bush Administration promoted a voucher system for parental choice, and sponsored the New American Schools Development Corp. to provide privately funded grants to design innovative campuses. The voucher system would provide $1,000 to help send low and middle income children to private schools. Critics point out that $1,000 might be helpful to those who can afford private schools anyway, but would not help those who cannot. American Federation of Teachers President Albert Shanker says, "There's not very much you can buy in education for $1,000 a year." ($1,000 would more than pay the per pupil cost of home schooling — which I discuss in just a few pages.) The Clinton Administration is opposed to the voucher system. So at least at the federal level, it's not going to happen any time soon.

"Choice" doesn't always involve voucher plans, or choosing private schools over public schools. Choices can also be created within a public school district, or even within the same school building. A most successful example of the schools-within-a-school concept is Harlem's District 4, which has experienced a complete turnaround under the program. "Junior High School 117" houses the Harbor

Junior High School for the Performing Arts, the science-oriented Career Academy, a special education unit for the handicapped, and the TAG School — a pre-kindergarten for talented and gifted students. Each of the small schools occupies a single floor of the school building.

In a few years, Harlem's District 4 has achieved astounding results. That district's schoolchildren have risen academically from last place among New York's 32 school districts to 15th, and the system of parental choices of innovative small schools has successfully spread to neighboring districts. Academic awards, scholarships and high scores on standard tests which would have been unthinkable a few years ago, are now regular occurrences. Groups that work for the kind of reforms that took place in Harlem include the non-profit Center for Educational Innovation and New York-based Manhattan Institute. Principals, reformers, and educators such as Lorraine Monroe, Joyce Duncan, Cole Genn, Leslie Moore, Mimi McDermott, Aileen DeFilippis and Sy Fliegel are some of the heroes of this New York success story.

In Minnesota, chartered schools are one new answer to the question, "What good is parental choice if all schools are basically alike and school boards have a monopoly on public education?" We saw in Harlem how innovation is possible within an existing school. Entrenched school boards and teachers' unions, however, generally manage to thwart that kind of independence and innovation. Grass-roots reformers have found other ways to innovate — successfully lobbying for state legislation, for example. While Minnesota has already had an open-enrollment system of choice for several years, a state law now grants broad powers to use public money in individually innovative and differing schools.

Allan Jones, a fifth-grade teacher who is part of a group that applied for a charter, aims to help his students develop problem-solving and critical thinking skills. He foresees many chartered schools using "seamless" teaching combining subject areas and encouraging student creativity.

Supporters of the charter system say that it is a results-based school system. The schools that produce the best results will thrive, and those that don't will disappear. The Minnesota law represents a pilot program, calling for just eight chartered schools, with no more than two per district. California has also passed a plan to develop 120 chartered schools.

Minnesota's pilot program of chartered schools seems most closely in line with the thinking of authors John Chubb and Terry Moe (*Politics, Markets & America's Schools*, Brookings Institution, 1990), who call for tax supported schools to be independently operated and to be in competition with existing school board operated public schools. Still considered public schools, chartered schools must meet general school board standards and must be non-sectarian and integrated. But they may serve the needs of special groups of students. In this plan, the operators of each chartered school decide how much local control to share with teachers and parents, if any. When parents choose a chartered school, the per pupil funding from the state goes directly to that school. By contrast, voucher systems provide for tax money to be given directly to parents to spend on tuition at the school of their choice.

Business Execs Turned Activists — A surprising number of successful business executives have become community activists and reformers combatting poverty and inner-city problems in general, and education problems specifically. In Chicago, Martin "Mike" Koldyke, millionaire founder-chairman of Frontenac Co., a venture capital firm, founded the Golden Apple Foundation which provides awards for outstanding teachers in the Chicago area. Koldyke has not only donated and raised money for the foundation, he has become profoundly involved in bettering education, especially for the poor. The foundation helps pay for the college education of those who commit to teach in economically deprived areas for five years. Koldyke also pioneered the program Teachers for Chicago to help people become teachers without having to give up their jobs. Through the foundation he is also working to get parks department personnel to keep school gyms open after school, and public-housing authority personnel to staff study halls in the high-rises.

His daughter says, "His measure of success has changed. It used to be 'How's the company doing?' or 'Do we have enough houses?' Now he's worried whether some kid's going to make it." Koldyke admits, "I still lead a pretty good life, but I'll never be able to go back to worrying about my golf handicap."

Martin Koldyke is not alone. Joe Kellman, chairman of Globe Group, an installer of replacement auto glass, started a corporate-community school in inner-city Chicago a few years ago. Similar stories are to be found in cities across the country.

Successful Blacks have formed volunteer groups in Washington, DC, and other cities, to return to inner-city schools as mentors and role models for young black male students. The early results are very promising.

In Kansas City, the late Ewing Marion Kauffman, who founded and made his fortune from Marion Laboratories, donated college scholarships to deserving, but impoverished, high school graduates of his alma mater. To receive the scholarships, students must not be on drugs nor have been pregnant, and must graduate on time with college-qualifying grades. The high school is in a low-income area with a 50% dropout rate, but Kauffman's legacy — Project Choice — is helping.

Businessman-turned-educator Steve Mariotti, founded and now heads a special education program used in New York's high schools called the National Foundation for Teaching Entrepreneurship (NFTE). The program includes hands-on training to inspire students to run their own small business, and helps them to get started. Some of the most "hopeless" young people have turned their lives around through this program, some forsaking the easy money of drug-dealing to instead sell watches, hats, hot dogs, colognes and school supplies. Boys Clubs of New Jersey has provided office space to NFTE, and grants from Citibank, Chemical Bank and Chase Manhattan, plus $300,000 from the Charles G. Koch Foundation have helped the program to expand to Witchita, Kansas, and to Washington, DC.

Stay-in-School, a non-profit organization started and led by Gerald Fields, a retired successful businessman, distributes thousands of posters to high schools each year, featuring such well-known cartoon characters as Bugs Bunny, encouraging students not to drop out. Some of the posters show the higher imprisonment rate of dropouts, while others compare the pay earned by dropouts versus that of high school graduates (the difference is dramatic — hundreds of thousands of dollars over a lifetime). The schools requesting the most posters since the program began five years ago show a 20% reduction in their dropout rates.

Education First, heavily supported by entertainment industry people, is also working on the dropout problem, educating the public to the fact that one million American students have been dropping out of school each year. They alert us, with literature and through the media, that 32% of American students do not complete high school and 80% of prisoners are high school dropouts. Education First's media people find subtle ways to work pro-education themes into their regular entertainment programs, in addition to their explicit public service announcements.

Private Scholarships for Elementary and High School Students — Incentives and support for students are on the increase. In addition to the well known multitude of college scholarships and financial aid programs for college students, there are a surprising number of private elementary and high school scholarships provided by the private schools themselves: 16 to 17% of all private school students benefit from full scholarships or substantial aid. This percentage has been increasing by close to one per cent each year for several years.

Volunteer Groups Recognize Student Excellence — For more than ten years, Links, an Afro-American women's organization, has honored young black men for scholastic performance and other abilities. All are college-bound, and some 330 of them have received Achiever award scholarships totaling $465,000 - with top awards of $5,000 each. The program includes psychologist-led workshops emphasizing sexual responsibility, discipline, self-control and ethical and moral development. One award winner in 1992, Tarlin Ray, a high school student body president, was accepted to Harvard University. Cosetta Moore, president of the Angel City chapter of Links, Inc., pointed out that "The mass media has showcased the negative views of young black males, but today we have a valedictorian, a poet, orators, church leaders. Individually and collectively, they are truly exceptional." Over 1200 people turned out to honor 1992's

33 recipients.

In another effort to encourage and recognize the academic excellence of young black males, the San Diego Urban League sponsored a luncheon to honor 200 young men with excellent grades at the end of the 1992 school year.

(As we go to press with this book in 1995, I realize that while some of the stories I've gathered have been updated, others haven't. But I believe the points being made would be exactly the same, and no book can take the place of the daily news media. The examples of grass-roots action are intended to acknowledge the specific people mentioned, as well as many others who could just as easily have been featured. Perhaps more important, these stories are intended as examples to inspire and motivate us all to do what we can to improve education in our own communities.)

Teach for America — Some volunteer organizations, while acting locally, are national in scope, such as Teach for America, a kind of educational domestic peace corps developed by Ivy League graduate Wendy Kopp. Volunteers, generally recent college grads, spend two years intensively helping the educational process in hundreds of under-staffed, inner-city and rural schools.

The Volunteer Role of American Business — Increasingly, business groups and large corporations have become activists to improve education. America's business leaders know that it is a matter of their economic survival in today's world marketplace to have clear-thinking, problem-solving, well-educated and highly skilled future workers.

RJR Nabisco has pledged $30 million over five years for its Next Century Schools program that funds experimental and innovative programs at individual schools across the country.

The Business Roundtable, an association of 200 of the nation's top corporate chief executives, has determined "that unless corporate America gets into...serious fundamental reform (of our educational system), we are going to be in the position of a declining country," according to Christopher Cross, the group's executive director. In Washington state, the Business Roundtable has succeeded in extending "Head Start"-type preschool programs to 100% of the state's income eligible children. These businessmen responded when studies showed that for every $1 spent on preschool the state eventually saved $6 in social costs.

Novel partnerships between government, public and private schools, and industry are on the increase. One example is Project Success at California State University at Sacramento, a program that offers under-represented minority students internship jobs with private companies combined with college education. Industry subsidizes the education, but gains good, ongoing workers and public recognition. Engineering and computer science Dean Donald Gillott and project director Jaime White are justly proud: minority students who previously had to work 20 to 30 hours a week to support their college education, which could then take six, ten, even more years, now graduate in four or five years. Best of all, these student-interns are virtually assured a job with their sponsor on graduation.

Some Public Schools Are Contracting Out — In education as in other matters, desperation breeds innovation. Miami Beach, Florida's South Point Elementary School, was the site of the country's first public inner-city school operated virtually independently by a private corporation. Education Alternatives, Inc., operators of private schools in affluent areas of Phoenix and Minneapolis, was hired to run the school for five years.

To make the plan feasible, Dade County had already given individual schools considerable autonomy, and the United Teachers of Dade agreed that graduate students could be used as part-time intern-teachers to keep costs down while providing one teacher for every 12 pupils. Every classroom was to have telephones and computers. To make this happen, Education Alternatives planned to raise $2.2 million over the five years from private foundations to supplement the normal public school budget. Since the company's annual fee of $200,000 to $250,000 comes from these donations, the private-public school experiment won't cost the school district anything extra. A low-income student population, mostly Spanish-speaking with below average reading scores, provides an adequate challenge for this experiment.

After one year's experience of running the Florida school, Education Alternatives was hired by the city of Baltimore to run eight elementary schools and one middle school for five years. By 1994, the contract included 12 schools. The private company will be allowed to spend the same $28 million the city would have spent directly on the same schools. For its part, the company guarantees efficiency and improved student test scores. EAI's chief John Golle vows to change schools that "look like prisons".

Late in December 1993, the Minneapolis school board hired Public Strategies Group, Inc., to manage the school district. The company's president was named superintendent.

An innovative and daring experiment to rescue a bankrupt and failing school district is underway in Chelsea, Massachusetts. Boston University President John Silber has led the university to enter into a ten-year contract with the local school board to run the city's schools. The contract, signed in 1989, specified that the only power the school board reserved was to fire the university. Silber, who had already greatly strengthened the university's finances, has raised millions of dollars for Chelsea's schools and has quickly succeeded in getting test scores up. He also has started an Early Childhood Program offering six pre-school classes for children between ages 3 and 5. The classes are open from 7:30 a.m. to 6 p.m. every workday of the year, including school holidays and vacations, enabling young mothers to go to school and work without being concerned about child care hours or costs. Silber notes that "Head Start still leaves out 40% of the eligible children" (not in Washington state, as we've seen), and his Early Childhood Program helps get the pre-schoolers ready to learn.

The Chelsea challenge was a great one. Not only was the district bankrupt, the dropout rate was over 50%, and most of the students are low-income minorities who speak English as a second language. A tireless worker to improve education, Silber would like to see schools teach the moral values of life to help counter what he believes are the negative effects of television.

Should We Teach Values in Public Schools? Do We Dare Not To?
— In California, the Irvine Unified School District has decided to

teach moral values. While for years public schools have not dared to teach moral values because of the close tie of morality to religion, the state has now opened the door with a change of rules. In Irvine, the school's board of trustees appointed a 20-member Values Task Force, made up of teachers, parents and members of the clergy. The task force came up with eight values to be taught, unanimously approved by the board: honesty, responsibility, compassion, perseverance, respectfulness, cooperation, courage and citizenship. Each school will be allowed to decide how to teach those values as part of regular courses.

Home Schooling — In greater numbers across America parents are turning entirely away from the school system — to home teaching. Many see home education as an opportunity to instill moral values, and religion as well. Conservative Christian homes probably account for 75 to 80% of home schoolers nationwide. Other parents keep children home because of fears for their safety, or simply because they believe their children will learn better at home. Today more than 350,000 children are being taught at home nationwide, compared to only about 15,000 as recently as the early 1980's.

Only some ten years ago parents were sometimes jailed for not sending their children to recognized schools, but grass-roots activists have prevailed on legislatures to ease up. Home schooling, with varying restrictions, is now legal throughout the country. The Home School Legal Defense Association, based in Falls Church, Virginia, assists parents facing legal challenges, and every state has home schooling associations. The average cost per pupil, about $400 to $500 per year (you see, $1,000 vouchers would cover two children), compares with about $5,500 for public and private schools.

Some public schools, as in Oregon, allow home-schooled children to use playground facilities, and even provide school supplies. There are private cooperative academies that teach courses such as advanced math, the sciences and foreign languages that are beyond what most parents can provide at home.

Standardized testing shows home-schoolers do as well or better than public school students, and about 50% go on to college, the same as for public schools.

FUTURE REALITIES

Certainly the future of education will include a continuation and enhancement of many of the reforms we have been discussing: local control, parental choice, more relevant curricula, and improved teaching methods. There may well be an increase of home schooling, parent involvement at school and at home, private school scholarships at the elementary through high school levels, incentive and mentoring programs, as well as innovative types of schools. Individual teachers and principals will continue to shine, and they'll get more recognition, awards and bonus incentives.

All of these changes are already taking place, but changes in our educational system will be faster and more sweeping as more and more people at the grass roots get involved in innovative efforts not only aimed at reform, but at more thorough transformation.

Many community activists, parents and educators advocate the increased teaching of values, accelerated academic programs, and the teaching of trades. Some are working to develop apprenticeship and internship programs off campus, and to establish schedules of campus visits by business, professional and other community mentors and role models, all as part of the curriculum. Such programs could give every student a head start in their careers.

In Chapter 6, I discussed how talk of change provokes our insecurities. As I tell you my plan for Accelerated Education which includes major changes, please remember that I'm going for great results. My intent is not to scare or to shock anyone, but to see those Big Issues transformed.

Why America Needs "Accelerated Education" — I'd like to see a huge grass-roots effort to accelerate the educational process. In recent decades, half of our children go on to college, and they ordinarily don't get there until they're 18 or older. State-run universities are overcrowded, with budgets strained to the max. At least half of the millions entering college never graduate, and the shear numbers on many state campuses have made getting a degree take five years, six years and even longer for those who complete the struggle for their diploma.

74

*All great truths
begin as blasphemies.*

— GEORGE BERNARD SHAW

JUMP-STARTING AMERICA

For millions of our young people, college is a wasteland of drunkenness and drugs, casual sex that belittles real relationships, and a stressful period of poverty that strains the whole family. Serious scholarship is the exception on most of our college campuses.

Sure, there are also thousands of students with high moral standards who don't succumb to today's amoral "norms". But, our system of prolonged years of education with its built-in poverty for most, encourages teenagers and young adults to have successions of short-lived sexual relationships. Do you think this is good preparation for developing committed relationships and families that last? Accelerated Education would be a force for strengthening the values that lead to stronger marriages.

It's hard on teenagers to be financially dependent on their parents even until age 18, let alone into their twenties (and even into their thirties and beyond in part because our present educational system omits serious vocational training), and it's tough on the parents, too. Our educational system simply doesn't prepare our children to be ready to earn a decent living upon graduating from high school at 18. This means that most of the 50% (half of all our kids who graduate from high school) that don't go on to college are only ready to earn the minimum wage. And those who DO go to college must usually wait until age 22 to 25 or later for a diploma to help them get a job that pays well.

Now that college graduates are so common, even they frequently fail to get other than menial jobs. In former times, until the last 20 years or so, a college diploma was still uncommon enough to have a fairly predictable economic value. In prior generations, when the vast majority did not go on to college, teenagers frequently went into the work force and often married before turning twenty. Divorce remained pretty uncommon until the 1960's, despite youthful marriages. And until recent decades, parents could count on their children to be earning their own living, be married and have independent housing by the age of 20 or sooner.

Our present educational system keeps our youth immature and unprepared for young adulthood. Since 18-year-olds can't make a decent living, they can't afford to get married. Half are untrained and the other half expect to go to college. So we see lots of casual sex, teenage (unmarried) pregnancy, sexually transmitted diseases, and boredom born of idleness that often leads to substance abuse and crime. Or at least leads parents to distraction. If teenagers knew they were being prepared to earn good money by age 18, many would look to get married at a much earlier age than we see today. This frame of mind would help prevent unmarried teen sex and pregnancies. And families would benefit financially and emotionally if most parents no longer needed to support children after about age 18.

As we all know, parents often try to use their control of money to control teen behavior. Conflict is inevitable, and the maturing process for the youngsters is put on hold. Earning sufficient money to live independently is a great force for maturity that is woefully delayed under our present educational system.

Poverty among teenagers and young adults is felt more acutely in our age of electronic gadgets and an endless list of consumer goods. Our kids, like the rest of us, aspire to a higher standard of living than people did in prior generations. So it's extra tough to be poor into the middle twenties or even older. And this system-caused poverty isn't necessary!

Shortening the number of years of schooling to permit economic productivity and independence at an earlier age, would have other beneficial effects: It would lower the cost of education and increase America's competitiveness in the world marketplace. It would discourage juvenile delinquency and reduce criminal behavior by teenagers and young adults. Financial success and marriage would give stability to the lives of young people and the entire community would benefit.

The Accelerated Education Plan — I propose that every student have the opportunity to be ready by age 18 either (1) to enter the work force with sufficient vocational skill and experience to earn a good living, or (2) to enter a professional school or academy to become a lawyer, dentist, physician, nurse, pharmacist, engineer, architect, physicist, chemist, economist, policeman, fireman, paramedic or other highly trained professional. This professional group includes all post-graduate degrees. Typically these professionals will have their

Love and marriage,
love and marriage,
Go together
like a horse and carriage.

— SAMMY CAHN

Marriage is popular
because it combines
the maximum of temptation with
the maximum of opportunity.

— GEORGE BERNARD SHAW

advanced degrees and will have completed their formal education by age 21 or 22.

And, with Accelerated Education, by age 18 all trades-persons, para-professionals, office personnel and business professionals (except MBA's) will generally be ready to launch their careers.

Elementary school will end with the fifth or sixth grade, and middle school will include seventh and eighth grades (and sometimes sixth) much as is true today in many, if not most, communities. The sixth grade could be either an elementary or middle school year, to be determined locally. The big difference in grade structure is that today's high school years will be replaced by college status for grades nine through twelve. Our present high school buildings will house junior (community) colleges, vocational schools, four-year colleges and academies. The greatest acceleration of education will come in the first eight grades, which would replace today's first TWELVE grades.

Accelerated Education will wipe out classroom overcrowding and school room shortages, and educational budgets will be showing surpluses where they now show deficits. Imagine the impact on costs by having shortened the years to a college diploma from 16 to 12! Savings nationwide could exceed 25 billion dollars annually within four years. Some of these savings could be used for improved facilities, and for higher pay — especially for the teachers and principals who achieve the best academic results. Most of the savings ought to benefit parents and students.

Some teachers and administrators will fear for their jobs, given the shorter pre-college curriculum. There will always be room for the best, and many teaching opportunities will be opened up as total parental choice leads to many new, smaller schools.

Critics will fear that students will learn less in eight years than in twelve. No way! Our children will learn MORE — for several reasons. The one million students who drop out of high school each year, and all of our other children, will all FINISH an eight-year program aimed at teaching all the relevant, currently 12-year, material. All our youngsters will also be provided with plenty of vocational and practical material that includes on-the-job training, experience and pay. The exciting pace of the eight pre-college years

79

will keep students alert, fascinated and attentive, rather than bored, distracted, and without hope or direction. Best of all, nearly all students will finish college or a vocational equivalent, and do it by about age 18. Dropouts will be rare in a setting of fast-paced, practical education that proves we're willing to let our teenagers have a life! A life filled with adult opportunities and responsibilities.

Our present junior college campuses will continue, but students will be accepted after EIGHTH GRADE (middle school graduation), the same as at colleges occupying former high school buildings. And our present major college and university campuses will also accept middle school graduates. College age students will be from about 15 though 18. Better colleges and universities (Harvard, Yale, UC Berkeley and Stanford, are examples) will still attract and accept the more academically successful and pre-professional students, just as they do now.

Student athletes will earn their college degrees by age 18 and could then turn pro! Why shouldn't our best athletes be able to earn a living at their chosen profession at 18, just like all others at that age? Today's college rivalries will continue not only at the undergraduate level, but at the graduate level. The UCLA Bruin Grads will duel it out with the USC Trojan Grads. So universities will still benefit from ticket sales and television rights, only now revenue will be generated at both the undergraduate AND graduate levels!

Let's face it. College sports teams really serve as unpaid minor league teams for the professional ball clubs today. Why not make it official and start paying those athletes (our youngsters) for putting up their skills and risking their bodies? Most athletes have relatively short professional careers, and could use the money over those extra four years. Of course, the professional clubs will have to decide whether to support the Grad teams, but I'll bet they'll do it if they get a split of the ticket and TV take.

Best of all, to make the Grad team, EVERY athlete must have earned her or his college diploma! What about women's professional sports? I'd like to see more of it, but the marketplace will decide. And the NCAA? They'll police college athletics as usual. Only, college athletes will be four years younger than at present.

Curriculum changes? You bet. First of all, no more repetition of many of the same courses in high school and college (no more high school). And no more reviewing for half a semester what was supposed to have been learned last semester, so typical of today's kindergarten through twelfth grade classrooms. Boring! Wasteful! And the repetition encourages slothful learning habits ("I don't need to work hard to learn it now, they'll only be teaching it again next semester anyway"). Let's add in lots of vocational training and off-campus apprenticeships and internships.

It's time to stop measuring the value of homework by its weight or volume. Kids need play, chore and work time after school, too. Make school and homework practical. Example: "Learn about interest by asking someone at home how much they still owe (the 'principal') on a car loan or other loan. (If they don't have a loan, make one up.) Ask for, or make up, the interest rate. Now calculate the interest that must be paid this month. Using the current total monthly payment and the portion of it that's interest, determine how much principal is being paid this month."

Every student will have part-time jobs, arranged in the community by schools working with cooperating employers, to take place during the school day. These jobs can be on- or off-campus. After several such experiences, which will start by age 12 to 14 (with parental consent), students will generally be able to decide on at least a first vocational career. Once a vocational choice is made, further jobs and training in the chosen field will be part of each student's curriculum, although changes can be made, until the end of college (now to be at about age 18). Students by the tens of thousands will have ready-made job offers from employers they have been learning from and working with during their school years. Having vocational training will not interfere with choosing an academic college program and even post-graduate professional training.

Courses in values, money management (covering budgeting, checking accounts, credit cards, loans, tax issues and investing), relationships and community affairs will all be either available or required (local control and parental choice being operative).

I favor using courses on practical subjects to also teach writing skills, math and reading, starting with the lowest grade levels. Instead of first grade readers with "See Dick run and see Jane play", we can have "See Dick look both ways before he runs across the driveway" (teaching safety), and "See Jane run to be on time" (teaching the values of reliability, dependability, courtesy and consideration). The next sentences could be, "If Jane is late, will you wait for Jane? How long will you wait?" (Here are concepts of time and the value of time, and we get into relationships, too.) It's still simple reading, but here are things to think about and discuss in class that deal with real life. Maybe we can do away with the barbed wire fences and truant officers if schools are made more interesting.

How will the transition be made to Accelerated Education, and how will it start? We'll only get Accelerated Education in America with massive grass-roots activism pushing for it. Parents, that means you and I have work to do. And the transition? Local conditions and local control will determine the details. Many of the curriculum changes can start at all grade levels, but the accelerated feature needs to begin with the older students.

Here's how it can happen: After the first year of an accelerated curriculum, those who have just completed their 11th grade will begin their first year of college along with the last batch of 12th grade high school graduates. The students fresh out of 11th grade can take that first year of college at their present high school campuses, and may have to if outside colleges won't admit them at this early stage of the transition. After the second year of an accelerated curriculum, those who have just completed their 10th and 11th grades will go on to college, whether we choose to call them "middle school" graduates or "high school" graduates. After the third year of an accelerated curriculum, those who have just completed their 9th and 10th grades will begin college. So, you can see that by the time the fourth year of Accelerated Education has been completed, all those completing the 8th and 9th grades will go on to college, and the four years of high school will have been eliminated. Just the years, not the learning.

Of course, we can call middle school "high school" after the transition, or the name "high school" can just be dropped. What matters most is the acceleration of our education process by four years so that 18-year-olds are ready for adult responsibility — ready

82

either for professional or advanced vocational schools, or for the workforce — fully trained, experienced and qualified for adult earnings. No longer will foreign kids be years ahead of ours. And our young people will finally be able to start out ahead, not behind, when it comes to worldwide economic competition.

The Edison Project — It is unclear whether new programs, still largely on the drawing board, will incorporate many of the Accelerated Education concepts. One of the most innovative and ambitious plans, the Edison Project, sponsored by Whittle Communications, aims to do nothing less than "reinvent the American school". Christopher Whittle, who heads the company sponsoring the Edison Project, launched *Channel One*, a system of classroom televised news, in 1990. Whittle is not afraid of the controversial nature of his educational reforms, having withstood some highly vocal criticism of his use of commercials in *Channel One* presentations.

Through the Edison Project, Whittle envisions building 1,000 new, for-profit private schools. Scholarships will be given to low-income students, who will make up 20% of the total enrollment of 2 million students planned by the year 2010. Costs will be reduced by replacing some teachers and aides with audio and video technology, having students (instead of full-time janitorial workers) clean the campuses, franchising cafeteria operations, and by markedly reducing administrative personnel. One goal of the program is to show public schools how to cut costs and improve learning.

To get this educational venture going, Whittle succeeded in recruiting a team headed by Yale University's president Benno Schmidt. The team includes: Brookings Institutions' John Chubb, who advocates total parental choice of schools; Chester Finn, Jr., a Vanderbilt University professor who served as assistant secretary of education under the Reagan Administration; and Sylvia Peters, the widely-recognized Chicago elementary school principal who is credited with transforming an inner-city school.

Whittle suggests the following scenario as a possibility for "the new American school": "A new school day might be eight or nine hours long to match the parents' workday. Two of those hours might be spent in peer learning groups, another hour in physical activity.

There might be two 90-minute sessions with an ELS (Electronic Learning System), individualizing and specializing a student's academic interests; two hours might be spent at an 'at-school job', learning skills and responsibility. And, believe it or not, teachers might actually be freed up enough to spend an hour or more every week or so in one-on-one work with each student." The plan provides for every student to have an ELS at home "with unlimited on-line access to an electronic library of books, films, speeches, lectures, and learning games."

In March of 1994, the Massachusetts Department of Education awarded management of three new schools to Whittle's Edison Project. The new schools are due to open in 1995 in Lowell, Worcester and Boston.

Privatization Plans — Other suggested innovations call for the chartering, privatization, or communitization of public schools. All are intended to bypass the vast administrative expense, wastefulness and inflexibility of governmental bureaucracy. All envision providing improved educational techniques and curricula with wide open parental choice and total local control. The likely results of the free marketplace provided by any of these schemes are: better educational results, economic efficiency, a weeding out of the least competent teachers and least needed administrators, and more funds for those most capable of providing good schooling.

Libertarian groups and others advocate a complete break with governmental control of public schools. For them, and for me, the answer is the privatization of schools. "Privatization" refers to the process of giving ownership or control of formerly public schools to non-governmental groups or to private companies, whether non-profit or for-profit. Under this program, governments could choose to rent the schools to such entities, or sell the facilities outright to them. With full privatization of a school district, state and local governments will no longer be involved in running or monitoring those schools.

I believe that, from a grass-roots perspective, the most compelling solution calls for the development of schools that are privatized so as to be operated by non-governmental, non-profit foundations organized by the grass roots. A community school system that REPLACES public schools will make moot arguments over whether private or public schools are better, and whether parental choice with vouchers could injure public schools. The community or "communitized" schools will use either the same existing school buildings and campuses that had been operated as public schools, or other facilities, depending on local circumstances. In most cases, the community foundations will rent the public school facility for a nominal fee from its governmental owner, and will always have total control of curricula and of the hiring of teachers and administrators.

The main difference between community schools and most non-religious private schools is that community schools will be non-profit and controlled by non-governmental community groups, rather than for-profit and run by private companies. I have absolutely no quarrel with private for-profit schools or parochial schools, and I much prefer all of these to government schools ("public schools"). Private and parochial schools could also rent former public school facilities. Full parental choice means that the free market will determine which schools thrive and survive. Chances are that the winners will be the best schools.

I'd also like to see the privatization of government-run community colleges and state universities, and with the current trend toward corporate partnerships for research and development, as well as corporate scholarship and internship sponsoring of students, all coupled with alumni support, the feasibility is clear. Partially, or totally, deferred tuition is preferable to government loans that too frequently end up as a taxpayer burden. Alumni, making repayment of their deferred tuition out of their earnings, would get used to sending money to their alma maters on a regular basis, so that their support might continue after their deferred tuition has been repaid (good seats at university concerts and athletic events make great added inducements).

Privatized schools, such as community schools, can be supported by private tuition made possible by vouchers or tax savings. For example, tax credits could be given to parents who educate their children outside the public (tax-supported) school system. For this system to work, most states (and most counties and cities) would have to pass laws and ordinances allowing parents a tax credit equal to the per pupil dollars that state and local governments spend on public schools. Parents could use their tax credit dollars to pay tuition to the community school or private school of their choice, after taking those credits as offsets against property taxes, and other state and local tax bills. Renters with school-age children could afford tuition by claiming refunds from the pool of property taxes, paid by landlords, that would otherwise be used to pay for the public schooling of the renters' children.

Under this tax credit system to pay for privatized schooling, state and local government budgets for public schooling would be markedly reduced, ultimately to zero. And the vast majority of parents could afford private or community schools. Private and community school scholarships would pay for the rest.

As a safety valve, some public schools could be maintained (remember how some people kept their horses and buggies for a while?), or government scholarship or voucher funding for low-income families could be provided, until the tax credit system, combined with private scholarships, is fully established.

When it comes to government vouchers or tax credits, I see no conflict with the First Amendment if parents have an unrestricted and complete choice of schools that are or are not affiliated with religious groups, even a choice of home schools. Choice is choice. If we restrict or limit choice, it's not choice anymore. It would be different if the government paid money directly to religion-affiliated schools or mandated that parents choose them.

Regardless of how it's to be accomplished, most school reformers favor the maximum possible degree of parental choice. Wide open choice is likely to result in healthy competition among schools — competition that in turn is likely to help control costs and to improve the quality and variety of education available for our children.

SPECIFIC ACTIONS YOU CAN TAKE NOW

If you're not already fully involved, and you find yourself inspired to become a volunteer or even an activist to improve education in America, you may find it difficult to pinpoint just how to begin. As you were reading about the activities and groups under way today, or those in the proposal or planning stages, you may have found one that "had your name on it." How do you start? It depends on your goals. I'll give you some examples.

A good place to start getting involved is in your own family or neighborhood. If you have school-age children there may be an aspect of your child's schooling you would like to help improve, either by working alone or within some existing group. You can begin at home by helping with homework, or at the school by mentoring, assisting in classrooms or on playgrounds, and organizing teacher recognition.

As a student, you can start a teacher recognition program, help improve the curriculum or the learning environment, or tutor younger students. Student and youth activism, fairly dormant for two decades, is resurfacing in responsible and creative ways.

Whether you're a parent, student, teacher or concerned citizen, you can help organize after-school activities, either on- or off-campus, or get involved in letter writing and other forms of lobbying. You can join the types of organizations you've been reading about (listed in this book's Index) or form one of your own.

Perhaps you would like to help organize a local community group of parents, teachers and others to work for the privatization of your area's public school or schools. Or, you can help form a group to advocate Accelerated Education.

Any of these involvements can bring you the satisfaction that comes from knowing you're working to create significant community-betterment.

Time will confirm or refute my view that education in America bottomed out in the early 1990's, and is on the way up. The possibility is at hand for magnificent new heights to be reached in the next ten years and beyond. Our dreams for American education will come true only because thousands, even millions, of us Americans not only want it to happen, we're willing to do what it takes to transform those dreams into realities.

Regardless of the diligence and enthusiasm of our involvement to improve education, the other four Big Issues threaten to limit our success. No single Big Issue exists in a vacuum. Each needs the powerful impact of our grass-roots revolution. For example, unless the problems of drugs and crime are vastly improved both on our country's campuses and off, many students' lives will continue to be ruined or cut short, teachers will be endangered and our efforts to improve the educational system will be slowed. The Big Issue of Crime and Drugs, which I discuss in the next chapter, provides another vital and challenging role for grass-roots activists.

8

CRIME AND DRUGS:
Winning with Peaceful Solutions

In recent years crime and drugs have become almost synonymous. Nearly one out of every 250 Americans is in prison today, and over 70% of the inmates are incarcerated for drug-related offenses.

Why don't THEY do something about it? THEY do. Our federal government spends more than 15 billion dollars a year on a mainly fruitless War on Drugs. Meanwhile, drug-selling gangs continue to shoot each other and innocent bystanders over valuable drug turf, and ten million dollars a day is being spent on building new prison space. It's Prohibition all over again, only worse. We would be better off if WE rather than THEY did something about our drug and crime problem.

At first blush it seems unlikely that we ordinary citizens can succeed where elected officials, law enforcement agencies and billions of dollars have failed. But let's bravely explore that possibility. There are innovative ways for all of us at the grass roots to make a difference, to get results using peaceful solutions that work, rather than warlike tactics that don't.

If Americans are as ready as I think they are to achieve huge reductions in drug-related and other crime, we will see that kind of improvement over the next ten years. We will see it, as Wayne Dyer would say, when we believe it, and I would add — when WE make it happen.

TODAY'S OBSCENE CRIME AND DRUG SCENE

In any society there is likely to be a certain amount of crime and substance abuse that, even under ideal conditions, is difficult to fully eliminate. Perhaps the America of the 1950's, for those of us old enough to remember, typified an era with "tolerable" crime and substance abuse levels.

Today more people are murdered in Washington, DC, than in any other "civilized" COUNTRY. Atlanta and Miami suffer about one crime for every five residents yearly, and a violent crime is committed against one of every 25 people. Most of our larger cities are not much better off.

So what's happened to the more peaceful America of the 1950's? Experts blame the crime increase on drugs. The War on Drugs has "created a new class of organized crime...more violent than the old organized crime because it's made up of more crime-prone people: young, disenfranchised kids," according to Gene Stephens, Professor of Criminal Justice at the University of South Carolina. And the bottom line is estimated to show that America's drug dealers take in over 100 BILLION dollars a year. According to Thomas Loreto, who supervises U.S. Customs Service teams specializing in confiscating drug money, "It's growing astronomically. It seems to be the one business that's completely recession-proof."

But why the big increase in drug use? We can point to the decline of healthy family relationships and the moral codes that are often a part of strong family ties. The decline of the family has many components: a huge growth of two-income households (no parent home with children after school), the sexual revolution, pervasive permissiveness, thousands of unwed mothers, abortions by the millions, and rampant divorce with innumerable "broken" homes (no father in the home, mother overburdened).

Another factor contributing to drug abuse and crime is

The common argument that crime is caused by poverty is a kind of slander on the poor.

— H.L. MENCKEN

poor inter-group relationships. Personal insecurities often lead to hate, prejudice and discrimination aimed at groups other than one's own. In turn, members of targeted groups often become insecure themselves, and more prone to drug abuse and criminal behavior.

In today's America, it is still largely unacceptable, especially for men, to talk about their personal problems and negative feelings. Besides our society's tendency to favor looking good over being good, men carry the additional unnecessary "macho" burden that "a real man goes it alone, no outside help needed or permitted." To many men, and women as well, getting drunk or "loaded" on drugs is more acceptable than talking things over with people they trust.

Some people say we have suffered a spiritual decline, a loss of values, or a failure to take responsibility. Whatever we choose to call it, or whatever we say has caused it, a social decline has taken place that has stirred up our human insecurities. The resulting pressures frequently reach the point where drugs are too often used for relief. And crime is the companion of widespread drug use.

Finally, the single most important factor in sustaining our current high crime and drug abuse levels has been our very belief that THEY, not WE, can, should and will somehow solve these problems.

THE WAR ON DRUGS "THEY" WAGE

"THEY", of course, are our elected officials, bureaucrats, "experts" — anyone but us. As the decades go by, we elect different politicians from the two parties, we spend trillions of dollars, we build more and more prisons, and we see the problem getting WORSE. When will we learn? Take a look in the mirror. You're looking at awesome power to make a difference, and you're looking at a reminder that WE are the only THEY who can succeed.

Let's examine what THEY are doing lately and the results they're getting. THEY are doing what they usually do. They're spending lots of money, passing tougher laws and pressing more and more law enforcement officers and bureaucrats into official action. They call it the War on Drugs.

The more they spend our money to suppress illegal drug use, the higher drug prices climb, which only entices more people to get involved selling them. Of course, addicts have a tougher time paying the rising prices, which encourages them to become drug dealers, prostitutes, thieves and robbers to support their habits.

When we tried a war on alcohol, called Prohibition, we had similar results. Illegal alcohol on the black market brought prices that created a whole new mobster industry of bootleggers and hijackers. For the Al Capones of that era, it was the criminal chance of a lifetime. When alcohol was finally re-legalized, mobsters could no longer profit from illegal booze. Alcohol abuse remains a problem, but not a gangster problem.

The amount of money now being spent in drug combat is vastly higher than the federal government's 15 billion dollars a year. Add in local and state law enforcement, court and prison costs. Then add medical care and funeral expenses for victims. Now add losses due to burglaries and robberies, plus expenses of auto accidents caused by people under the influence. Then add the rising costs of health and auto insurance due to these drug related accidents. To these add the welfare costs of caring for the families of imprisoned, unproductive or dead drug abusers, and the families of their victims. The sum is in the multi-billions, virtually incalculable.

And that's only the money.

What about the damaged, destroyed and wasted lives? What about the thousands of hours of jury time that jurors could better spend? And the fear that keeps law abiding citizens off the streets, locked in their homes? What about the innocent bystanders shot by drug gangsters, even grandmothers and babies shot by bullets crashing through the walls of their homes?

If Drug Wars were being won, all of these costs and tragedies would be steadily dropping. But we see that they are either increasing or remaining at intolerable levels.

Advocates of the War on Drugs tell us that we're winning because drug prices are getting higher, because cocaine is not as easy to buy as before, because we have more drug offenders in prison than ever before, and because we're confiscating more tons of drugs than ever.

Many people, including me, believe that these same facts prove the failure of Drug Wars, not its success. The government assumes

When a stupid man is doing
something he is ashamed of,
he always declares that
it is his duty.

— GEORGE BERNARD SHAW

Nothing in life is so exhilarating
as to be shot at without result.

— WINSTON CHURCHILL

Reprinted by permission of ROGER LUTEYN

that higher prices show the effectiveness of drug interdiction by law enforcement. Yet higher drug prices might also reflect a higher demand. These higher drug prices, whatever the cause, make drug dealing more profitable. And, have you ever heard anyone say that they would be using illegal drugs but they are not doing so because the drugs cost too much? On the contrary, addicts do whatever they have to do to satisfy their habit. The higher price of cocaine is part of the same picture. High prices may discourage a few casual users, but this benefit is outweighed by the enticement of profits to be made from those higher prices.

More drug offenders in prison only proves that the problem continues to grow. In the Vietnam War, increasing enemy body counts did not indicate impending victory, as some of our leaders claimed at that time, but rather, indicated the entry of more and more enemy soldiers into the battle. Similarly, the confiscation of more and more tons of illegal drugs only indicates that more and more drugs are being smuggled into the country. Law enforcement has never been able to capture more than a tiny percentage of the drugs flowing in, or the drug money going out.

Our policy of Drug Wars has only succeeded in driving the illegal drug market a little further underground, if even that. For example, a 1990 survey of high school seniors found that cocaine and marijuana were less readily available, but the survey didn't ask whether there was any REAL DIFFICULTY in obtaining them.

There is no evidence that cuts in supply really exist or, if they do, that shortages have altered anyone's drug habits. It is clear that illegality itself, and the mighty arm of the law, has not stopped anyone currently using drugs. Even prison inmates obtain illegal drugs, and many more resume their habits upon release.

Not every drug user is willing or able to push drugs sufficiently to pay for their own habit. Often addicts resort to crimes such as burglary, theft, robbery (with or without violence), prostitution, embezzlement, forgery and fraud — as economic backups.

Among all of today's grim realities, are there no bright spots, no positive forces already in action to reduce the toll of crime and drugs in America?

SOME RAYS OF LIGHT

The crime and drug problem is so severe as this is written in 1994, that it's hard to believe that any bright spots exist. But they do. They are mainly the reparative activities of grass-roots organizations, some of which receive governmental financial support.

Reparative activities include numerous transitional housing programs to help the homeless rejoin the mainstream. A high percentage of the homeless being assisted have histories of severe substance abuse problems, including alcoholism. Many are on parole for drug related offenses. Although transitional housing programs have paid staff, volunteers play an important part, and many more are needed.

In my own experience as a volunteer with various transitional housing organizations, mostly leading support group meetings, I've been inspired by the progress of many of the residents. Some alumni have gone from parolee drug offenders, alone, broke, homeless and jobless, to fully recovered status — including independent living with families, jobs, cars, even their own businesses. Recovered addicts are now "sponsors" in Alcoholics Anonymous or other "anonymous" organizations, helping others to recover. Former jobless and homeless people now routinely assist others in obtaining work and housing. Several transitional housing groups report rates of over 90% of their residents going on to independent housing and jobs, but recidivism is still high.

More volunteer mentors and support group leaders are needed. If you've never hit rock bottom in your life, it's hard to know just how tough it is to get back on your feet. And, if you've never had the experience of being of service to people in this position, it's just as hard to imagine the joy you can experience in doing so. This is definitely an example of where the distinction between giver and receiver is blurred. I found that I can never give more than I receive in this work.

It's important to help people pick up the pieces of their lives that are hopefully only temporarily "broken". But reparative work alone is not enough. Bad and broken relationships often lead to drug and crime problems, poverty and homelessness. Still missing are the innovative grass-roots activities that will help our communities have the strong, thriving families whose members are emotionally secure, have high self-esteem, and who benefit from top notch educational programs and job opportunities, and good inter-group relationships. Where these conditions prevail, crime and drugs don't, and won't.

Many grass-roots programs, while not new or innovative, have for years served as a positive influence: Big Brothers and Big Sisters programs, Boys and Girls Clubs, Scouting and YMCA/YWCA are just a few of the established vehicles for those who wish to get involved. Many of these programs provide positive after-school and weekend activities that help young people avoid trouble. As wonderful as these programs are, they are obviously not nearly enough to combat our crime and drug problems.

The Drug Policy Foundation headquartered in Washington, DC, is a group hard at work searching for alternative strategies to Drug Wars, and educating all of us on the subject. The organization is headed by two American University professors: Arnold S. Trebach, president, and Kevin B. Zeese, vice president and counsel. As their brochure says, the organization was formed in 1987 "to combat the drug war hysteria and to advocate sensible ways to curb drug abuse and preserve everyone's constitutional rights...it is time to treat the drug problem as a public health problem, not a criminal justice problem...We are not far from the day when government officials and private employers will have the legal power to require any citizen to urinate or defecate in front of witnesses. The Drug Policy Foundation wants to help prevent that day from coming."

The organization also educates the rest of us about the prohibitions against legitimate medical uses of drugs that are otherwise illegal. Its excellent publications present the case in favor of the government allowing these uses.

For example, marijuana prevents the severe nausea and vomiting that accompanies most courses of chemotherapy for cancer. No other known drug can match marijuana for this purpose, and marijuana has been baked into brownies, especially for children, so it doesn't have to be smoked. Marijuana reduces eye pressure in some glaucoma cases that are unresponsive to other therapy, and is also known to relieve spasticity due to multiple sclerosis. Heroin relieves pain for terminal cancer patients better than legal narcotics such as morphine, and doesn't cause nausea. In recent years the government has stopped allowing even the few medical exemptions to doctors that they formerly allowed, and patients suffer accordingly.

The Drug Policy Foundation is an innovative grass-roots organization that deserves our praise and support. I am proud to have been an associate and a member of its Science and Health Committee. Its laudable efforts alone, however, can't be expected to bring peace to the chaos of Drug Wars.

Similarly, all of our drug treatment and preventive programs, "Just Say No...", methadone clinics, social work and other counseling programs have all failed to significantly reduce our overall crime and drug problem.

It is not my intent to criticize existing grass-roots efforts. They are mostly wonderful and if anything need to be increased. It IS my intention to point out that bravely innovative and transformational grass-roots efforts on an unprecedented scale will be needed for us to get the results we want.

THE RESULTS WE ALL WANT

Just what is it that we hope to accomplish with regard to crime and drugs? I think most will agree with the majority of the goals I'm going to name, but some readers might take issue with some of the results listed here.

Safe neighborhoods and safe streets are something we all want. We want our children to be safe at school, and while going to and from school. We need more people with high self-esteem, with access to good education, jobs and careers. We need more families of the "nuclear", or traditional type, and we need them to be LASTING families. And households of all types, conventional families or otherwise, need relationships of unconditional love and support between all who share their lives. My son Jeff puts it this way, "We need fewer houses and many more homes."

In my hometown area of Los Angeles, nuclear families are rare enough that when my wife, grown children and I enter a restaurant, I sometimes sense that the other patrons are scrutinizing us with visual Geiger counters — "Whoa! Don't look now, but here comes a NUCLEAR FAMILY!" Just by being together, we are unusual. Our strangeness is only enhanced by the fact that we appear to be enjoying each other's company.

Imagine America with many more millions of loving and stable families, so that more of us will have the emotional strength not to get into drug abuse and crime.

We need better inter-group relations that open doors of opportunity to all and help keep community peace.

Our schools need to be so effective and inspirational, and so connected to career development, that every 18 year old has the opportunity to be ready either to earn a living that will support a young family, or to go on to professional training.

Our country needs to medicalize, not just criminalize our substance abuse problems. Drug and alcohol abuse need to be seen as social and health problems, and not just as matters for the criminal courts and prisons. Drug treatment programs are terribly inadequate and must be innovatively improved. Education about drug abuse is way off target. Doctors and patients, not laws and bureaucrats, should be able to determine and carry out drug treatment programs.

We want much less drug abuse, we want drug dealers out of business, and we also want fewer people arrested, on trial and in prison.

We also want to stop the rampant spread of AIDS, hepatitis and other diseases by shared needles, and by promiscuous and unsafe sex practices.

Quiet and peaceful communities mean lower, not higher body counts, arrestees, prisoners and drug confiscations. Lower, not higher drug prices, will signal substance abuse abatement. Lower, not higher government spending to combat drugs and crime, will indicate that significant improvement has occurred.

INNOVATIONS WE NEED NOW

To get the results we want, massive, and well-aimed grass-roots activity will be needed. Volunteerism works best when it can work directly, without having to work for passage of new laws to permit the effective activism. However, in the case of drugs and crime, some activists may want to work for at least one new law, through lobbying, letter-writing campaigns and by backing or opposing specific lawmakers. It isn't that we can't be effective without the new law, it's that the new law will allow our work to bear fruit more quickly and easily.

We need Congress to pass a new law relating to drug access for addicts, to treatment of drug abuse and to the use of otherwise illegal drugs to treat diseases. I call it the "Regulated Substances Act", a sample text of which appears in Appendix A.

You may find it hard to believe, but it's true that current law emasculates physicians, preventing nearly all of them from treating drug addicts if treatment is to include any LEGAL, controlled substance. Certainly we don't want doctors to be glorified drug dealers, selling narcotic prescriptions to addicts in the false name of treatment. But today only authorized methadone clinics are allowed to use narcotics to detoxify and/or maintain addicts on narcotics. This monopoly allows the exploitation and mismanagement of the addicted patients.

I propose that the Act permit all physicians to prescribe otherwise illegal drugs such as marijuana and heroin for their cancer chemotherapy and other patients, or legal narcotics such as methadone for narcotic addicts. Informed consent of the patients would be necessary, with the physician bearing the professional responsibility. The physician would be required to write a treatment plan in the patient's medical record that explains how the treatment is intended to benefit the patient.

Besides dealing with medical treatment, the Act would provide for a legal and well-regulated means for addicts to obtain their drugs so inexpensively (no dose over three dollars) that street dealers are put out of business. Confirmed, regular drug abusers and addicts of at least 21 years of age could obtain the same drugs they already had been buying on the streets. Illegal drugs confiscated by law enforcement would be used for this purpose. No doctors' prescriptions would be involved. There must be sufficient time between purchases so as not to invite overdoses or street sales. Sharing or selling of drugs by authorized purchasers would be strictly illegal. All street sales, sales

Squeeze human nature into the straitjacket of criminal justice and crime will appear.

— KARL KRAUS

Reprinted by permission of ROGER LUTEYN

to minors and all sales to anyone not possessing the DEA (Drug Enforcement Agency) identification card authorizing pharmacy purchases would be illegal.

The law would also provide amnesty for dealers and possessors of illegal drugs who come forward to turn in their inventory, including illegal weapons, and who agree to permanently stop dealing drugs.

The reason for offering amnesty is to get dealers to quickly quit the business once the new law has made it entirely unprofitable anyway, and to get into custody any remaining illegal drug inventory and illegal weapons.

To get amnesty, these persons must agree not to name or accuse anyone else of being a drug dealer or user. This way former customers or other dealers who choose not to seek amnesty will have no reason to be suspicious of, or to take revenge against, those receiving amnesty. Amnesty will allow the former drug dealer to convert to a "normal" life without having to look over his or her shoulder, and without burdening the judicial system with a myriad of cases concerning ex-dealers.

The good news is that dealers not seeking amnesty will soon have no profitable business anyway as their former customers sign up for regulated drug doses at no more than three dollars a dose (see Appendix A).

In January, 1990, I sent a copy of my proposed Regulated Substances Act to a fine gentleman and distinguished American, George Shultz, former U.S. Secretary of State and now at Stanford University's Hoover Institution "think tank" as an Honorary Fellow.

Shultz was chosen with good reason. He had already shown the courage to publicly announce his view that entirely new alternatives need to be found to our present Drug Wars strategy. In 1989 Shultz publicly stated, "We need at least to consider and examine forms of controlled legalization of drugs." Here is his reply to me:

"Thank you for your note of support for my statement about America's need to take another look at how we deal with the drug crisis. I feel confident that public opinion will eventually fall in behind a more balanced and sensible approach to drugs. The illogicality of present policy seems clear: we have created by law a vast market in which profits are gigantic; we have then said that all those who operate in that market are criminals; and we then put enormous resources into driving them out of the market. The market is too rich and the incentives to create new addicts too great. So the market has to be dismantled if drug use is to be diminished. At the very least, the issue should be examined with care.

"Thanks also for sending your proposed 'Act'. It looks most interesting. I agree with you that 'regulation' is a better word than 'legalization.'"

"Regulation" is a better word because I am far from advocating outright legalization of any illegal drug. "Legalization" implies a more wide open situation. In the case of alcohol, for example, there is far less control than what I propose for illegal drugs: registration of habitual drug users with ID cards, strict limitations on quantity purchased, required educational video sessions, and strict price and distribution controls.

George Shultz and I have lots of good company sharing our point of view. I am pleased that other officials, including Baltimore Mayor Kurt L. Schmoke, Federal Judge Robert W. Sweet, Superior Court Judge James P. Gray, and retired New York Chief Detective Ralph Salerno (who headed the real-life *French Connection* heroin bust) have all called for changes in our approach to illegal drugs and the associated crime, that are similar to my proposed Regulated Substances Act.

This proposal is a far cry from outright legalization. And it is a far cry from the total illegalization and Drug Wars that we have now.

THE BENEFITS OF "REGULATING" ILLEGAL DRUGS

There is much evidence to cause us to believe that this form of regulated, restricted legal availability would lead to decreased, not increased, drug use, and lead to lower crime rates.

The first type of evidence is the decline of the use of three legal

Reprinted by permission of JOHN TREVER

106

substances in the USA: tobacco smoking, distilled spirits (whisky, scotch, vodka, gin, etc.), and glue-sniffing. In each case effective health education and publicity have helped create these declines while sales of the substances remained legal.

Ironically, tobacco and distilled spirits, which cause hundreds of thousands of American deaths each year, remain legal, while all the illegal drugs combined kill fewer than 8,000 Americans annually.

A second piece of evidence that legal access to drugs by addicts would not cause an increase in drug use comes from a 1990 survey by Targeting Systems, Inc. A random telephone poll of 1,401 adult Americans showed that if marijuana were TOTALLY legalized, only 1.1% of those who hadn't tried marijuana said they would be very likely to try it. Of those who said they HAD tried marijuana, only 8.5% thought they would be very likely to try it again if legalized. For cocaine, the figures were even lower — 0.5% and 1.5% respectively. As an aside, this same survey revealed that by more than 3 to 1, Americans prefer treatment and counseling for drug users caught possessing drugs rather than fines and imprisonment.

The third piece of evidence comes from the Dutch experience. Although the same drugs are illegal in the Netherlands as they are in the USA, their government rarely punishes drug users for possession. Instead, the Dutch authorities offer treatment on demand, encourage needle exchanges, teach heroin addicts to smoke dope rather than inject, and turn the other way as marijuana is sold in coffee houses quite openly. The results? The Dutch have FAR LESS illegal drug use per capita than we have in the USA, and AIDS is very rare. Half of their narcotic addicts no longer even use needles, having learned and chosen to smoke their dope. One result of the soft handling of marijuana is that marijuana is not sold by the same dealers who sell heroin and cocaine, which is often the case in the USA. This may be the very reason why harder drugs are less used by the Dutch.

In other European countries who conduct Drug Wars more or less as we Americans do, illegal drug use and AIDS are far more common than in the Netherlands, and resemble the figures in the USA. So the Dutch experience is not a European versus American phenomenon. In fact, only Britain, which generally shares the Dutch approach of "harm reduction" rather than imprisonment and strict law enforcement, has similarly better statistics of drug abuse and AIDS. What some might criticize as excessive leniency by the Dutch government has produced these impressive numbers: Only 0.15% of the Dutch are drug addicts compared to over 5% of the USA population!

It is clear that tough law enforcement, or Drug Wars, is not synonymous with lessened drug abuse. It also seems reasonable to believe that when the prices of illegal drugs are so low that addicts need not commit ANY crime to obtain their drugs, all crime will be reduced. Certainly the crime of pushing drugs to others to raise money for one's own drug habit will disappear. With fewer pushers around, fewer neophytes will be tempted to try hard drugs. Without the dealers on the streets, the people of our communities will not only feel safer, they WILL be safer and once again be able to take pride in their neighborhoods.

Also, with profits from street sales removed, why would the drug cartels continue to import drugs into the USA? Who would their buyers be? If their only remaining illegal drug market will consist of sales to minors and to neophytes, drug dealing will no longer compete favorably with "regular", less risky jobs and businesses.

Once illegal drugs are made available to addicts very inexpensively in a regulated manner, what incentive would there be for young people to join drug-dealing gangs? With profits gone, there would be no drug turf to fight over, no more "drug deals gone sour" with bodies everywhere. The need for expensive undercover law enforcement would virtually disappear. With very little new drug quantities coming into the country, there would be little to interdict, few drugs or drug dealers to "bust".

The whole idea is for our grass-roots movement to help bring peace and stability to our streets and neighborhoods, to contain the currently out of control drug and crime problem. The notion that with sufficient troops, firepower and money, we can deal a total knockout punch to the drug and crime problem is both wrong and dangerous. Drug Wars has already led to a kind of civil war in our streets — profiteering gang versus gang, and all versus the government's law enforcers. If we keep escalating Drug Wars, we could soon have troops and tanks on our streets. The body counts will go up, but we'll still have the problem, and those bodies will be us! We need peace, not war.

ACTIVISTS AT WORK

Already grass-roots activists are breaking the law in some cities, and causing new ordinances to be written in others, as they bravely go out into the streets to conduct exchanges of clean needles for dirty ones, so that drug addicts won't spread AIDS, hepatitis and other illnesses.

A Yale University study in 1991 showed that a needle exchange program in New Haven, specially permitted by the Connecticut legislature, reduced the spread of HIV infection by a third in just eight months. New Haven's Mayor John Daniels said, "This program is not a solution to AIDS or to drug addiction. It is one more *Band-Aid* but...it is a *Band-Aid* we cannot afford to do without. It works...we have really reduced tremendously the spread of AIDS in the city of New Haven..."

I would add that for those who would have been infected from a dirty needle, and for those sexual contacts of addicts who would have been infected later, the prevention of AIDS was more than a *Band-Aid* — it was transformational. AIDS is only going to be defeated by two methods: prevention or cure. Either method transforms the AIDS situation.

Edward Kaplan, an associate professor at Yale who ran the New Haven study reassures those who think needle exchanges promote drug use, "A needle exchange program does not change the number of needles in circulation. It increases the turnaround. The length of time any given needle lives on the street goes down. The number of injections per syringe must decline, reducing the chance that the syringe becomes infected. The risk of exposure to a needle contaminated with the HIV virus is lessened." The average time for a marked needle to be returned for exchange dropped from 2½ weeks to six days.

New York City ran an exchange program for a while under Mayor Koch, but Mayor Dinkins didn't continue it. Needle exchanges

109

are operating in Hawaii, Seattle, Portland and Boulder, Colorado. Police seem not to be interfering with still illegal needle exchanges in San Francisco, New York or Los Angeles unless there are citizen complaints. In Los Angeles, an unofficial Clean Needles Now group reaches only about 150 addicts who can exchange dirty needles for clean ones. But there are an estimated additional 190,000 illegal needle users in LA County still sharing dirty needles for weeks at a time. And at least six percent of them are HIV positive.

One fascinating side effect of the New Haven program was that 100 of the needle recipients entered drug treatment programs, and 100 more were waiting for openings. This positive reaction of the addicts to non-threatening contact with "authorities" who care is reminiscent of the Dutch experience. The New Haven response is a strong hint that soft, peaceful handling of illegal drug use, treating it as a medical and social issue rather than primarily as a criminal problem, will work in the USA.

While we await new laws and ordinances, there is much that community activists can do. Churches have been used as "safe houses" for many causes, and have been used for needle exchanges. At safe houses, addicts can be encouraged and educated in smoking dope rather than injecting it. Safe houses can be used as places where drug dealers who wish to get out of the business can come to turn in their illegal weapons and drug inventories. Volunteers working in the safe houses can destroy the weapons and can distribute the drugs at no charge, with the help of volunteer doctors and nurses, to adult addicts who are otherwise committing crimes to feed their habits. Counseling, medical care, and drug treatment programs, including detoxification could also be carried out at these safe houses. There may be such safe house efforts already underway, but for obvious reasons, there hasn't been any publicity.

These daring and positive safe house activities that I advocate need not remain dangerous and illegal forever. Once the public and lawmakers see that neighborhoods with safe houses are becoming safer and freer of drug dealers and related crime, it will be easier for us to obtain the laws we need to really transform the entire drug and crime problem for our whole country!

Why don't our senators and congressional representatives pass, now, the laws needed to curb drug street sales, and to allow needle exchanges? Congressional aides have told me that our elected officials are afraid. They're afraid of losing their next election, and they're afraid of drug lords coming after them if they support any legislation threatening to wipe out their lucrative drug industry. Only massive grass-roots support for such legislation can eliminate those fears and turn things around.

Our present drug treatment programs don't generally deal with why drug abusers use drugs. This subject doesn't get the attention it deserves in our educational programs for young people in school or for adults. People at the grass roots who work with substance abusers can help change this. Doctors, nurses, social workers, psychologists, MFCC's (marriage, family and child counselors), and teachers can start spreading the needed messages.

Those messages are: (1) Drugs (including alcohol) are so dangerous because they WORK, especially at first. If drugs didn't relieve pressures and tensions, if drugs didn't produce euphoria and highs, why would anyone bother to use them? So the first thing everyone needs to realize is that drugs are so dangerous because they provide the user with relief, at least in the short run. It is easy to see why drug users believe that they truly NEED drugs for relief. It is easy to see why people turn again and again to the drug that gave them relief in the past. (2) All of us have negative feelings. Given enough negative feelings of sufficient power, relief becomes a necessity. There are only three ways we can get relief from the mounting pressure of negative feelings held inside of us: (A) we can go crazy in one of several ways — using violent behavior or speech, truly going insane or committing suicide; (B) we can use drugs or alcohol to get relief, to get that euphoria or high that for the moment helps us to escape any awareness of our emotional stress; or (C) we can verbally express our negative feelings to someone we trust, our support person or group. This will lead to our receiving empathy, advice, or, most helpful, a challenging question such as, "What are you going to do about your problems?" As we answer, we find ourselves heading in the "normal" direction of coping, taking steps to end the problems causing the negative feelings in the first place.

Use of these simple messages has led people to see that they have a choice, that they don't really NEED drugs. And this same information can be used to help people learn to cope in ways that will prevent drug abuse in the first place. Compare this method to "Just say no..."

Many communities are experimenting with alternatives to imprisonment for people arrested for possession of illegal drugs. These alternatives include drug treatment programs, counseling and community service activities. Grass-roots volunteers, people like us, can write letters to local judges, help form treatment programs for arrestees, and write letters to the editors of our local newspapers to encourage these practices.

Today there are a great many programs, scattered and fragmented, to work with underprivileged, inner-city and minority youth, but there is very little coordination between programs. As a result there is lots of duplication of efforts. Also serious is the lack of easy access to information for people who want to get involved as volunteers or even for those who want to benefit from these programs. Here and there are mentoring programs. A few hundred children in every large city have Big Brothers or Big Sisters. Some join Scouting, go to Boys Clubs and Girls Clubs, enjoy YMCA/YWCA activities or recreational programs at city parks.

These scatterings of programs cannot possibly cope with the magnitude of young people that need to be reached and contributed to in ways so consistent and meaningful that individual lives and whole communities are transformed.

A VISION FOR THE FUTURE, STARTING NOW

I envision a volunteer program I call "Project Miracle" for every city and town that wants it. This would be a comprehensive program that acts as a networking center for all mentoring, tutoring and positive activities groups. Sponsors from the business community and other private sources will sponsor youth athletic teams and leagues. Project Miracle will not only coordinate these athletic activities, but will also find sponsors to reward academic improvement and excellence, to award prizes to essay contest and scientific exhibit contest winners, to provide scholarships, to offer summer job programs as well as internships, apprenticeships and permanent jobs.

Project Miracle will hold fund raising and award picnics or dinners once or twice yearly, and the organization's goal is to be a positive influence on the life of every school age girl and boy that the organization can reach. The idea is to provide youth with so many positive activities and directions, that delinquency and gang activities will simply be ignored or rejected. Existing groups and facilities will hopefully play a cooperative role, such as YMCA/YWCA, Boys Clubs and Girls Clubs, Girl and Boy Scouts of America, and cities' departments of parks and recreation.

Specific goals include an athletic team opportunity for all who want one, a tutor or mentor for all who need and will accept one, and academic, job and career counseling equally available.

Each city's chapter of Project Miracle will add its name to the organization, such as "Project Miracle New York" or "Project Miracle LA".

ACTIONS YOU CAN TAKE NOW

Eldridge Cleaver said, "You're either part of the solution or part of the problem." When it comes to getting involved to produce community-betterment, there is no neutral ground. You're either involved, accomplishing and being fulfilled or you're not. I hope you're getting your share of that satisfaction and joy.

Beyond mere involvement is another question. Is your specific activity making enough difference for the time and effort you're giving?

Take a look at how your work is or is not affecting the OVERALL status of the issue you care about. Could you be accomplishing more, even transformational results, by switching to, or adding on, a different activity? If you're doing only reparative work, I'm inviting you to experience the innovative efforts capable of preventing and eliminating whole categories of problems while bettering lives and communities.

The issue of crime and drugs is in desperate need of our transformational grass-roots help.

So what actions can you take now?

Before primary election time, you can find out how the candidates stand on needle exchanges, on regulated and inexpensive drug access, and on treatment for addicts. You can do whatever you can to help elect any candidate willing to go public with favorable views on these issues.

Between elections, you can help organize a ballot initiative or write letters to your state legislative, congressional and senatorial representatives, and the President. It's much more effective to organize a letter-writing campaign than to send only one letter, even if that letter has several signatures. Elected officials pay more attention to outcries that seem widespread in their district, and not just the workings of a single group. So why give the false appearance of a small group or committee?

One common technique for a letter-writing campaign is to write two or three sample letters that make your point, and give copies of them to your friends, family and co-workers who share your viewpoint. They can then paraphrase your letters slightly, requiring very little time or effort, and they will appreciate your supplying them with the names and mailing addresses of the elected officials. And your contacts can pass on copies to their contacts. Don't collect letters so that they can be sent in one packet! Many separate envelopes make a bigger impression, as do letter-writing campaigns sustained over several weeks or months.

Petitions can be effective too. Your elected representatives have to be impressed by the signatures of hundreds or thousands of voters in their district.

The role you currently play in society may provide you with activist opportunities not readily available to everyone.

Health care professionals can work through their organizations, and can try to gain consensus in talking with colleagues. For example, professional health care associations could be effective in calling for legalizing clean needle exchanges, and for educating addicts regarding inhaling dope rather than injecting it (to prevent the spread of AIDS, hepatitis, and other diseases). Just as urgent, medical professionals can push for the legal prescribing of otherwise illegal drugs to treat diseases, and the right to prescribe legal

114

narcotics as part of drug treatment programs for addicted patients.

If you're a legislator, you can introduce legislation legalizing needle exchange distributions. Joseph Galiber, a State Senator in New York, introduced legislation similar to my proposed Act, to provide a regulated means for addicts to legally obtain their drugs. Members of Congress, you can have the same courage!

If you're an attorney or a judge, you can help build support for alternative sentencing of addicts arrested for possession of illegal drugs. And attorneys know that they have a special ability and duty to defend the Bill of Rights against violations by Drug Wars zealots.

If you're a member of the clergy, consider letting your house of worship be used as a safe house, at least for clean needle and syringe exchanges.

Are you a law enforcement officer? Perhaps you can discourage and avoid random searches and wildcat break-ins that you wouldn't want done to you or your family. Some of those break-ins cause severe damage to the wrong homes and even the killing of completely innocent people.

And there are more actions that ANYONE can choose: Would you like to help organize a Project Miracle in your city? Do you have the courage to get involved in safe house activities? Even if you don't personally exchange needles or accept illegal weapons or drugs at a safe house, you could be considered to be aiding and abetting criminal activities.

You might be a "criminal", but only in the same sense that those who hid Jewish children from Nazi extermination were criminals. Treasonous colonists defied the King's laws during the American Revolution. And then there were those who broke the laws of southern states to help Blacks escape slavery by heading north. Not bad company for the stout-hearted.

A step we can all take is to begin to think of each drug abuser as a human being with serious problems: an inability to cope with negative feelings, and legal and health problems. Only this outlook allows us to help instead of punish. We must remember that whenever we punish or lash out, we are also punishing ourselves. So we need to limit our punishment to truly dangerous perpetrators, because the rest of us must always bear costs and consequences. Can we damage an addict's life with stiff legal penalties without other lives being damaged (the addict's family, tax costs for all of us, and victims in the community between imprisonments)? Can we help an addict without the whole community benefiting (reduced law enforcement, incarceration and health care costs, and fewer secondary victims)?

Right now, we all can begin to think of drug abusers as real people with names and relatives — as people who, besides being likely to end up very sick, dead or in prison, may have positive possibilities if we can find ways to help them turn their lives around. Our new attitudes, our new kind of drug education, and the new laws we'll get passed will be great for starters!

Then there is the personal level we can each deal with: Are our own noses clean? A most apropos question in our current cocaine age, or should I say "rage"? We have seen political leaders, athletes and other celebrities participate in anti-drug campaigns in public or on TV, only to be uncovered later as drug users themselves.

Drug use and abuse is so ubiquitous that very few of us, if any, can say that neither we, nor any member of our families, nor any close friend has had a substance problem. All of us can work to have the kind of self-relationships, and relationships with others, that tend to prevent the trap of substance abuse and crime (see Chapter 11).

Even crimes that are not drug related are also associated with emotional insecurities. Always we find the same lack of self-esteem and the inability to cope with perceived mounting internal pressures leading either to substance abuse for relief, or to violent or "crazy" behaviors that are crimes when innocent victims result. Here is where a Warm Line volunteer system (see Chapter 10) can help transform our social environment to prevent many of these terrible results.

Right now you can find out more about the Drug Policy Foundation based in Washington, DC, and if you like what you learn, you can join as I did.

Right now you can help organize letter-writing, petitioning and lobbying to get the Regulated Substances Act passed. This will be the biggest giant step for mankind since before the Eagle landed. Thousands of lives will be saved. Billions of dollars can be better

Bottom Liners

3-30

"Soledad! Camarillo! Attica! Folsom!... When are we finally going to settle down, Ronald?"

spent, or saved. Our streets will become much safer, virtually free of drug dealers and related crime.

Only OUR personal involvement can produce these results. If you identify crime and drug abuse as one of YOUR issues of concern, you can gain fulfillment by getting into action NOW.

Yes, WE can and WE will be effective in reducing crime and drug abuse. WE will help find, choose and elect candidates dedicated to bringing peace to the chaos of our crime-ridden streets in today's Drug Wars.

People DO recover from substance abuse. Not always on the first try. But what an accomplishment it is! And how proud people should be when they become at peace with themselves, and attain the unconditional self-love and coping abilities that allow them to remain clean and sober for many years at a time, if not for life. WE can be those people. WE can participate in the recovery of people around us, in no small part by giving them our unconditional love and encouragement, and by providing a legal and medical environment that favors recovery. WE can help build a society too healthy emotionally and too secure to be caught up in significant drug abuse or crime.

9

CURING OUR HEALTH CARE SYSTEM:
The Community Health Association

While our medical scientists win Nobel Prizes, some 37 million Americans have no health insurance, and most of the rest of us can barely afford it. On top of that, millions of Americans are doing an awful job of taking care of their own health, and much of the health care dispensed to those of us who ARE insured is inefficient, inappropriate, just plain incorrect and dangerous.

As this is written, Congress is considering the Clinton Administration's health care proposals, which threaten to toss our health care system from the frying pan into the fire. The prospect of a massive new governmental health care bureaucracy is, in itself, a health care crisis of greater proportion than the one we already have. This is not about President Clinton. No matter who is in office, we've learned that when THEY swing into action, our troubles get worse, not better.

Worst of all, a government takeover of our health care system will rob all of us Americans of a splendid opportunity to run a great system of health care from the grass roots. I'll describe that system, which I call "CHAP", in just a few pages.

Let's face it. The government can't point to a single area where it's been economically or administratively efficient. For example, some estimates point out that only about fourteen cents of every Medicare dollar goes for actual patient care. The rest pays for the bureaucratic wasteland. And if we have to depend on government officials to approve our care in advance, we'll all be "covered", but we're not likely to be cared for WHEN we need to be. A person with a three-month life expectancy unless heart surgery is done, will probably go on a nine-month waiting list.

Privacy regarding our personal health, and real choice of health care practitioners and facilities, will be non-existent. And while doctors and drug companies will be paid less, health care will cost all of us much more in taxes, debt dollars and poorer health.

At least today, good and timely care is available to SOME Americans. Will the grass roots stand by while THEY make sure all of us can enjoy the same, equally inferior health care service?

Today, though, we do in fact have serious health care problems. Some aspects really DO constitute a crisis, but they're not the ones getting all the press. I'm a physician with experience in private practice, and I've worked in city, county, university, veteran and military hospitals. More importantly, I've been a patient, too. So, when it comes to health care issues, I've had plenty of first hand experience to serve as background for my views.

Whether the issue is health care or any other issue, each of us decides to get involved to help make a difference, or to sit back complaining that THEY ought to do something. This chapter aims to inspire widespread grass roots activism, on an unprecedented scale, to solve America's health care issues by organizing Community Health Associations and by implementing its health care plan, the Community Health Association Plan, or CHAP.

THE LACK OF HEALTH CARE ACTIVISM SO FAR

But, far from the situation we find with regard to such Big Issues as education and the environment, grass-roots activism (aside from lobbying groups) has not developed to improve our health care system through direct actions to implement innovative plans. Instead

The single most exciting thing you encounter in government is competence, because it's so rare..

— DANIEL P. MOYNIHAN

That government is best which governs the least...

— THOMAS JEFFERSON

JUMP-STARTING AMERICA

Reprinted with special permission of NORTH AMERICAN SYNDICATE

we have seen valuable volunteerism in terms of hospital helpers, support groups for patients and families beset by many ailments, and disease-specific charities which have raised vast sums of money for care and research. But, as valuable and necessary as these activities continue to be, grass-roots innovative activism to improve our health care system has been sparse. So, guess what? The problems are only getting worse.

Perhaps THEY have been counted on too heavily on this issue. THEY have brought us Medicare and Medicaid programs which have certainly not solved the problem of affordability. And further government-based programs are bound to be as costly and budget-busting as we can imagine in our worst fiscal nightmares. Do you believe that quality of care and economic efficiency will be produced by new laws and new bureaucracies? Will enough of our most qualified young people want to become government-regulated health care professionals?

But THEY are not limited to elected and appointed officials. Large insurance companies, HMO's and other people involved in "managed" or contract health care companies, medical associations such as the AMA, and hospital associations have all been counted on to provide answers. THEY are all around us, and have been for years — and yet our health care crisis is still all around us, too, and growing.

As our wisest leaders have frequently reminded us, no widespread American problem is ever really solved without widespread American involvement. Grass-roots activism has begun to produce significant improvement in environmental issues and in education. Health care also needs to be improved from the bottom up rather than from the top down.

TODAY'S HEALTH CARE CRISIS

For us to get a grip on what we should and can do at the grass-roots level, we should first take a look at what the health care crisis is all about as this is written in 1994.

Affordability and cost are the same problem viewed from opposite sides. As costs increase dramatically, affordability diminishes. Lower the costs, and you get more affordability, which also improves accessibility. But in addition to affordable cost, accessibility requires availability as well. Even if costs are low enough, what if adequate facilities and personnel aren't available in a particular area? This unavailability can be due to the absence of facilities and trained personnel, or it can mean the presence of facilities that are misused even by adequate numbers of well-trained personnel. Unfortunately, the latter has become a common condition even in our largest cities, and even for fully insured patients.

The misuse of health care facilities and personnel takes two forms: (1) In the pre-paid (HMO) sector, we often have serious undertreatment of patients. Why? With fees collected primarily in advance, all the economic incentive for HMO health care organizations is to give as little care as possible. Profits and end of the year bonuses depend on how much money is <u>not</u> spent on patient care. (2) There is rampant inappropriate overtreatment in the fee-for-service sector, which includes privately insured, as well as Medicaid and Medicare patients. Why? As insurance companies and governmental payers try to control costs by reducing fees paid for each service, health care professionals all too often respond by doing unneeded operations and procedures to maintain their income levels. Besides, patients tend to go along with more office visits, tests, procedures and operations when the bills are going to be paid by someone else. This system of distant "third party" payment for health care has resulted in unethical practice and massive increases in costs.

Doctors are paid the same office visit fee, for spending 20 seconds with patients, that they would get for spending 20 minutes. All of the incentive is to quickly order a bunch of tests and procedures, for which the doctors are often able to collect fees. It's also easier and more profitable to quickly (and prematurely) write a bunch of prescriptions for potentially dangerous drugs. After all, if you get side effects, you'll just need another office visit to deal with them. And if tests and procedures are ordered, you'll need further visits to go over test and procedure results. Too many health care professionals have sold out to this costly, unethical and dangerous way of taking advantage of today's system of distant third-party payers.

Curing Our Health Care System

125

In fact, America's health care costs are rising at 11% a year — about four times our overall inflation rate! No wonder thousands more of us flock to county hospitals and go on Medicaid programs each year. No wonder millions of us can't afford soaring health insurance premiums, while millions more pay the premiums only at great sacrifice. No wonder millions of children go without needed care, and adults do likewise.

What's going on here? Are greedy doctors, laboratories, drug companies, pharmacists, hospitals and health insurers engaged in a conspiracy to gouge the public? No, not a conspiracy. But there are far too many instances of over-pricing, and of doctors and dentists performing unnecessary operations, procedures and tests. Despite these unsavory practices, reduced third-party fee schedules and the overhead costs of malpractice insurance and billing have reduced the standard of living of most physicians, dentists and pharmacists over the past ten years. And nurses are chronically underpaid.

What's going on is that more money is spent on administrative and peripheral costs than on actual patient care. What's going on is that these spiraling costs have removed millions of people from access to preventive care and to early care for serious illnesses. What's going on is that the breakdowns in our society are resulting in huge medical costs for treating victims of violence, substance abuse and sexually transmitted diseases. What's going on is that those same moral and ethical breakdowns explain why many health care professionals dispense unneeded and inappropriate care for financial gain, regardless of who may be hurt.

There's no question that people are eating, drinking, smoking and drugging themselves to death, as part of today's "breakdowns in our society." While we perceive that physical fitness is "in", obesity and lack of adequate physical activity are rampant, drug and alcohol abuse are ubiquitous and the HIV virus continues to be spread through sex and shared needles. And what's the use of working out at your local gym, only to be mugged by a drug addict or killed by a drunk driver on your way home? Poor self-care and violence are major factors in today's runaway medical costs.

As technology has improved, too many doctors and hospitals have purchased the new technological equipment and now must use it enough to pay for it. Sometimes many offices in the same building, and many hospitals within a small area will have the same equipment at great cost. Inefficiency abounds. A single medical building with forty offices has forty reception rooms, of course. If there are forty internists' offices in the building there will be forty electrocardiograph (ECG) machines, and in some areas, almost as many x-ray machines, laboratories and technicians.

In response to soaring costs, health maintenance organizations (HMO's) and large clinics have emerged to provide efficiencies. But impersonal contract-care and overcrowded clinics are rapidly becoming the norm, and big city hospital emergency departments have unconscionably long waiting lines. Frequently HMO patients don't get the care they need promptly enough or even at all, and rarely do people have a choice of physicians. The quality of medical care, and the quality of the medical care experience, are too often lacking.

Political parties and elected officials have offered ideas for reform. The Democrats have suggested that employers either furnish health care insurance or pay for government coverage. The Republicans have called for tax credits for health insurance. Neither of these proposals will combat the rising costs of care at all, and it is questionable whether these plans will significantly improve accessibility.

For example, no matter what health care financial demands are made of employers to pay for employee health coverage, there will always be millions of unemployed, and therefore uninsured, people. Many small businesses will go out of business if forced to provide major health care funding for employees. And why should employees be tied to their jobs because of health insurance? Obviously, tax credits won't help the unemployed buy health insurance.

Managed competition can succeed in lowering costs, but only when it's not part of a governmental bureaucracy. Even then, the slight lowering of costs carries the price of people not being able to choose their own doctors and hospitals, and not being able to obtain sufficiently personal, considerate and prompt service.

Quality of care, wellness promotion, and illness prevention are generally not being effectively addressed. America's newborn survival rates are shockingly poor compared to other "civilized" countries, and

A government which robs Peter to pay Paul can always depend on the support of Paul.

— GEORGE BERNARD SHAW

The nine most terrifying words in the English language are, "I'm from the government and I'm here to help."

— RONALD REAGAN

129

our rates of HIV infection and substance abuse rank at the top. Infants and children frequently go without needed care.

Prescription drugs are increasingly unaffordable, and often are not covered by insurance. Even if insurance were to cover medications universally, the cost of health insurance would simply become still less affordable.

Today, prescription writing is at a maniacal pace, and a major health care cost is the treatment of side effects and serious complications from the use of drugs, tests and procedures that were never needed in the first place. Some 20% of hospital in-patient days are devoted to treating illness DUE TO MEDICAL TREATMENT!

Is there anything, then, in our health care system that we might want to keep? You bet there is.

OUR CURRENT HEALTH CARE STRENGTHS

America's medical technology is the best in the world. We invent 55% of the world's new drugs. People who are able to do so, almost invariably choose America for life-saving therapy requiring advanced surgical techniques and equipment.

Concern for life and for recovery from illness has always been the hallmark of the vast majority of American health care professionals. Many thousands of our health care professionals are dedicated, honest and caring, and practice their healing arts with great integrity and skill. And we must recognize the scientists who invent new treatments and equipment, and those Nobel Prize winners who make the scientific breakthroughs.

Every major city has its free clinics, and its doctors and nurses who frequently donate their services. We are inspired by stories of American doctors, nurses and other health care personnel traveling thousands of miles to assist earthquake victims in Armenia and Latin America, and nuclear plant disaster victims of Chernobyl, without any financial compensation.

In cities all over the country, thousands of citizens donate money to replace stolen wheelchairs, to pay for the tests needed to identify compatible organ donors, and much more. Volunteer blood donation, as well as organ donation, are marvels we now mostly take for granted. Nearly every sizable hospital depends on an army of volunteers.

Paramedics responding to "9-1-1" calls save lives every day that would otherwise be lost. Pharmacists warn patients about possible drug interactions. Many people try to improve their diets and work out regularly — sometimes in facilities provided at the workplace. Many thousands have kicked substance problems such as smoking, alcohol, hard drugs and food abuse.

Volunteer organizations exist to counter the ill effects of virtually every known ailment. These organizations promote research and treatment, provide education, and support the families of those afflicted. Yes, healthy loved ones need support, too, and this need has sometimes provided the impetus for "ordinary" people to accomplish the extraordinary.

Jim Segel's wife had Alzheimer's Disease. Her mind was gone, and although she was still alive, Jim had already lost her companionship, but not the continuing burden of her care. In despair, Jim found and attended a support-group meeting. He discovered people with stories as sad as his, some worse because of a lack of financial resources for the care of stricken loved ones.

Soon Segel had helped organize what has become the nationwide Alzheimer's Association with some 1,600 support groups and 207 chapters. The association provides families and caregivers of patients with emotional support, practical help and information (for example, regarding adult day-care centers), and encourages research and advances in treatment. Segal's wife died some time ago, but he remains active in the organization, raising funds and helping the loved ones of Alzheimer's victims cope.

Candy Lightner experienced grief and anger when her daughter was killed by a drunk driver. Lightner managed to channel these emotions into constructive action by starting Mothers Against Drunk Driving (MADD). It is probably true that the heightened awareness of the problem of drunk driving produced by the activities of MADD and similar organizations has saved lives, saved many severe injuries and saved the families, of those who otherwise would have been killed or injured, from major anguish and expense.

Scientific wizardry! Marvelous technology and equipment!

Dedicated and skilled professionals! Accomplished activists and volunteers! Yes, we do want to maintain our health care strengths and build upon them. We must do nothing, in our zeal to improve our system of delivering and paying for health care, to damage these outstanding qualities.

THE COMMUNITY HEALTH ASSOCIATION: THE FUTURE IN OUR HANDS

We must improve our health care system. Few would disagree. But how?

As we've noted, adding new government coverages and bureaucracies are sure to "bust" our budgets causing either major deficit increases, higher taxes, or, most likely, both. Massive government programs are not noted for economic efficiency and citizen satisfaction. Local control, local involvement and choice, obviously so important in education, are just as important in health care, and massive federal bureaucracy tends to destroy local control, local involvement and real choice.

Putting medical professionals, hospitals or the insurance companies in charge of reform would not be likely to result in much reform.

Fortunately we have one place left to turn to for relief. Yes, it's true. Once again, WE are the THEY for whom we have been searching and waiting. It's up to us to come to our own rescue.

After numerous discussions with health professionals, all of whom are patients at times, too, and with many others, I am ready to recommend massive grass-roots participation to establish, on a nationwide basis, the Community Health Association and the Community Health Association Plan (CHAP). I will use "CHAP" to describe the association and its plan interchangeably. CHAP challenges the conventional wisdom that health care must be controlled by government, insurance companies, hospitals or health care professionals, to the exclusion of the rest of us. With CHAP, the system is controlled by the entire community, every community, with plenty of local control and participation. And all without direct government involvement.

Curing Our Health Care System

Can government play a key leadership role in promoting the establishment of CHAP throughout the land? Very definitely! Might there be an important role for health insurers? Yes. Do we need the enthusiastic participation and leadership of health care professionals, hospitals and other institutions? Very much so. But can CHAP happen without massive grass-roots participation? Not a chance.

Let's take a look at how CHAP would work. With CHAP, the health care system is controlled by the entire community. Every member has a vote, and everyone can become members. Directors are elected at local levels, and each professional category monitors itself via elected peers. Regional and national boards are to be elected by local board members. What we have here is health care democracy in action.

CHAP will add no costs to government or to taxpayers, and will save such costs in the long run. CHAP could prove to be very effective in helping lower the cost of prescription drugs. The pharmaceutical industry has already indicated its willingness to limit price increases to the rate of inflation. CHAP could go even further, by being a major wholesale buyer of pharmaceuticals so that pharmacists who are CHAP health care professionals can sell at lower prices to CHAP members. Also, CHAP could be effective in getting pharmaceutical companies to sell equal quantities of pharmaceuticals at equal prices throughout the world. This would result in MUCH lower prices in the USA. If necessary, CHAP could lobby Congress to pass legislation forbidding price discrimination based solely on country of sale, for any pharmaceutical company marketing its products in the USA.

Health care costs can be drastically reduced by CHAP in several ways. The association will arbitrate cases of alleged malpractice involving its members. Health care professionals will share facilities and equipment. Standards of care will be set by professional peer elected representatives. Insurance forms and collection costs will be all but eliminated by an automatic, but audited, credit card type of payment system controlled by CHAP.

While CHAP will be a third party payer, it will be a LOCAL third party payer with local monitoring and control. Financial incentives and recognition will be built-in to assure that health care professionals are rewarded for the best health outcomes obtained with the greatest economy. This combination of local monitoring and built-in incentives will tend to eliminate unnecessary and absurdly brief office visits typified by plenty of unnecessary tests, injections and risky prescriptions.

Better health and better health care in the community can be promoted by CHAP in other ways, as well. Professionals with a record of multiple losses in malpractice lawsuits won't be admitted as CHAP professionals. And those CHAP health care professionals who are found to be significantly negligent will be removed from the system. CHAP will promote better self-care by its members through educational efforts that will include one-on-one personal contact. This will be helpful because such a high percentage of illness and injury are preventable. For instance, AIDS is a 100% preventable illness, yet is uniformly fatal, devastatingly brutal and terribly expensive if not prevented.

Appendix B provides a complete description of CHAP. Clearly the plan is likely to be altered as more people's ideas and suggestions come into play. But no matter what improvements are made to the plan, and no matter how promising any of us might find CHAP to be, America will never benefit from it unless hundreds, then thousands, of grass-roots activists help organize Community Health Associations which will then be able to offer the health care plan I call CHAP.

SPECIFIC ACTIONS YOU CAN TAKE NOW

You may be already involved as fully as you want to be in voluntary activities related to health care, or you may have other ideas, quite different from CHAP, that you wish to pursue for solving various aspects of the health care crisis. The purpose of this book and this chapter is not to divert you from your choices, but, rather, to encourage you to pursue those choices.

If you are sufficiently interested in the Community Health Association concept to read Appendix B, you may also be ready to get involved in starting an association in your own community. Chapter 12 presents some methods of organizing for results.

I'm available to assist anyone who contacts me at the address listed in the AFTERWORD, with regard to organizing Community Health Association chapters. I can supply information regarding progress in your area or nearby communities, and if others from your area have expressed an interest in CHAP, Project Jump-Start will pass that information on to all networkers, including you.

A good way to start is always within your own circle of acquaintances including your family, your work place and all health care professionals you may know.

Informal conversations can lead to structured meetings, planning, further networking and finally the formation of a pilot program in your area.

If you decide to take on being part of the CHAP evolution, be prepared for the usual roadblocks. There may be some well-meaning members of your family, and friends, who will tell you that it can't be done, that certainly YOU can't do it, who do you think you are, and why don't you give up this foolishness and stop wasting your time. And, as we'll discuss in Chapter 12, you're likely to encounter other obstacles, too. It's all par for this or any other course you will ever decide to play.

But you will reap the joys of success if you resist every temptation and excuse to quit. And, there will be the joy of being in action to get your desired results, to sustain you along the way.

Meanwhile, here's to the health of us all!

10

OUR PERSONAL ENVIRONMENT:
The Job Begins With Us

The Community Health Association, that only we can organize, will certainly be concerned about how our environment affects our health. Naturally, we must also be concerned with how we affect that environment, which is so capable of turning on us and causing us harm.

Some of the people deeply involved in environmental issues only care about protecting and enhancing the non-human environment from the harm done to it by people. They are much less concerned with the environment's effects on us humans. Nor are they concerned with the personal environment we create for ourselves. These people emphasize that man has no right to adversely impact the rest of nature. Period. Pretending that we humans, with our needs and aspirations, don't exist — or wishing that we didn't, is too out of touch with reality. It's a weird and extreme perspective which, by its nature, is anti-human.

Others, like me, are concerned about the effects of a damaged environment on people AND animals, and the rest of nature as well, but their emphasis is on creating or maintaining an environment that

137

will be good for people today and for future generations. Preservation of clean rivers and lakes, protection of forests and clean air, and recycling are all seen as practical measures to better OUR lives, while they are also good for the general environment, including animals and plants. But! At all times people come first, taking into account the long-range outlook for people. This is a perspective I can live with. What do you think?

Each us is free to choose our own set of environmental values, and then to decide how active we will be in supporting our views.

ENVIRONMENTAL GRASS-ROOTS ACCOMPLISHMENTS

Many Americans are convinced that our world's ecology continues to deteriorate alarmingly. At the same time, perhaps because of perceived danger, individuals and organizations at the grass roots are working hard to reverse the trend. Public environmental awareness is at record levels. For example: in homes and offices alike, recycling is the norm or is becoming so.

Environmental activists have achieved a great deal. Besides the massive growth of recycling, many species have been protected, Pittsburgh's air is much better, and even the air in Los Angeles is measurably cleaner. Leaded gasoline is virtually gone. With volunteer activist leadership, many corporations have cleaned up their environmental act, and "good corporate citizenship" is a recent concept that many companies aspire to.

Several beaches have been "swept" clean by thousands of volunteers, and the "Adopt-a-Highway" program is a successful example of government/private sector partnership to help the environment. Grass-roots activism is definitely responsible for tougher anti-pollution laws passed in recent years.

During California's six-year drought that ended in 1993, an aware and responsive citizenry conserved much more than the amount of water asked of them by officials. It was a remarkable grass-roots achievement that generally both preceded and exceeded government mandates. Some might argue that higher costs for water were responsible, but once again, Southern Californians were voluntarily conserving at maximum levels before the higher rates went into effect.

"STANDARD" ENVIRONMENTAL ISSUES

Today's environmental discussions tend to center around certain issues that are continually and repetitively brought to our attention. These are favorite media issues, so it's a familiar list: holes in the ozone layer, global warming, disappearing rain forests, polluted air and water, scarcity and hazards of landfills, endangered species and habitats, and a few others from time to time.

There are scientific controversies regarding the seriousness of holes in the ozone layer and the chances of global warming.

There are even controversies about recycling of newspapers, glass and plastic based on costs and concerns over possibly dangerous chemicals used to remove the newsprint from the paper.

But, there is little disagreement about some environmental issues: recycling aluminum cans, cleaning up old toxic dumps and controlling new ones, conserving water and other resources, and protecting our air and waters from pollution.

CONFRONTING OUR PERSONAL ENVIRONMENT

I'm not denying the importance of grass-roots efforts with regard to at least some of the "standard" environmental issues. However, this chapter's main focus is on the personal and local aspects of the environment. This approach is somewhat novel, and it may prove controversial. But I'm committed to this approach because it can lead to transformational grass-roots activities that can be a major part of our efforts to jump-start America.

That's right. I'm treating the environment as a PERSONAL issue. My goal is to successfully encourage innovative grass-roots activism that will encourage each of us to deal with our personal environment. When I say that cleaning up our environment "begins with us", I'm not referring to a need to get involved in the kinds of "global" issues we hear about every day. I'm quite literally talking about our personal environment, starting with our own bodies, minds and relationships. And when we have dealt successfully with those issues,

I suggest we next tackle improving our homes and yards, then assisting our neighborhoods.

After dealing with our personal and very local environment, we can move on to community and even worldwide environmental issues. To me this is a logical order or progression. I'm not suggesting that anyone give up their global outlook or efforts. I'm just reemphasizing the well-worn motto, "think globally, act locally", and when I say "locally" I'm referring first to the area inside your own skin. That's as local as you can get.

Some of these local, personal issues are very serious. Hundreds of thousands of us Americans die of smoking and alcohol related illnesses every year, vastly more than die of AIDS, illegal drug overdoses and dozens of rare, but well-publicized and financially addressed diseases, combined. Of course all the causes mentioned are worthy of our attention, but are we paying attention to the personal pollutants that are statistically most likely to kill us? For example: obesity (not mild overweight) contributes to the ill health and premature death of millions of us every year.

It's fair to say that, in addition to illegal drugs with all their harmful effects, Americans take more legal prescription and over the counter drugs than any other nationality. It's well known that a great many symptoms and illnesses are produced by legal drugs. We also drink water from taps that are too often putting out excessive lead or are contaminated with harmful bacteria.

This brings up the whole area of home safety. How many homes have fire extinguishers, and how many have reliable smoke alarms? Many homes have flaking paint with harmful lead levels, or acoustic ceilings with asbestos fibers.

On the neighborhood level, how close is the nearest toxic waste dump site? Are we in an area of high radon levels? Is our neighborhood (and our house) infested with rodents that can carry diseases, or are we endangered by locally high crime rates? Have lives been lost because there is no crosswalk or stop sign at a nearby corner? Do our local schools provide a safe and good learning environment, or do they just represent daytime dangerous prisons for our children, who can't wait to drop out?

Back to our most personal environment. How are our relation-

*The preservation of health is a **duty**. Few seem conscious that there is such a thing as physical morality.*

— HERBERT SPENCER

ships? Do you relate well to yourself? That is, do you accept yourself with unconditional love? Is your self-esteem level high enough? Or are you lacking in self-love to the point that severe insecurities are leading you into depression, substance abuse, and difficulties in relating to others, holding down a job or building a career? Just think how many Americans suffer from a lack of supportiveness from within and from without, from both their internal and external environment.

From without? Yes. All of us need a support group or at least a support person, someone with whom we can share our everyday good and bad. Relationships, and specifically supportive relationships that work, are dealt with more fully in Chapter 11. For our purposes now, let's acknowledge that it's better to live in a supportive environment than in one that is not, and that too many of us lack a sufficiently supportive environment.

You say you're too busy as an activist fighting pollution to pay much attention to your personal environment? That's up to you. But, let's use a little imagination to check out the results of ignoring the personal approach. Let's say you're a member of a group of dedicated grass-roots environmentalists who are just returning home from a meeting with corporate officials. At the meeting, the company agreed to reduce the amount of pollutants discharged into the air and into a nearby river. Happily your group of volunteers stops at a local restaurant for lunch. But as you all sit and eat, chortling deservedly over your accomplishment, some of you light up cigarettes. Or, at least, you all breathe the smoky air from half a dozen cigarettes in the restaurant's nearby bar. Over the years, these exposures can take their toll.

Yes, "think globally, act locally" — make that VERY locally.

GRASS-ROOTS WORK THAT'S NEEDED

So much has been written about existing environmental organizations, their accomplishments and the thousands of dedicated volunteers involved, that it would be redundant to review them here. I simply want to acknowledge their good works, and invite them and you to consider taking part in some innovative grass-roots efforts that America needs today.

The Community Health Association, as envisioned in Chapter 9 and Appendix B, would make a perfect organizational vehicle for very local and personal environmental work. But if the personal environment is your main issue, and you want to get started now, a small ad hoc committee may be your answer. You can always merge it into a Community Health Association chapter later on.

The kinds of community schools envisioned in Chapter 7, some of which essentially exist in the form of chartered schools, would include the teaching of healthy relationships with oneself and with others, in their curriculum. Any school, public or private, could do the same, but school boards may be difficult to convince. Good self-care can also be taught in schools, and at home.

The idea is that people with the highest self-love and self-esteem are least likely to damage their own lives, whether with pollutants one can smoke, drink or eat, or by mental pollution with negative thoughts leading to crime, depression, other emotional ills and even physical diseases.

The "Warm Line" — You know what a Hot Line is. These are the phone numbers people can call when they're having a severe problem or crisis, just one step below calling 9-1-1 for an emergency. Hot Line operators are usually volunteers. Some help teenage runaways, others help the suicidal, and so on.

So, local committees of neighborhood volunteers can also volunteer their Warm Line services to their neighbors.

But what the heck is a Warm Line? Warm Line services work in both directions. Neighbors are contacted by Warm Line workers who identify themselves and ask permission to inquire as to the well-being of the person and/or family called. Neighbors can also call a Warm Line volunteer to gain a supportive ear and to obtain assistance. The idea is to create a neighborhood environment of warmth, of support and assistance WAY before the situation deteriorates to the Hot Line or 9-1-1 stage.

It may take a while for people to get used to the idea that neighbors care about neighbors; and, not only do they care, they are ready, willing and able to assist. It may be a bit of a shock at first, especially in our big cities.

What are the goals of Warm Line volunteers? Every household in America is to receive a call once a month (more if needed and wanted) from a Warm Line volunteer, including the households of the Warm Line volunteers themselves. On site visits (house calls!) will be available upon reasonable request, and will be offered when it seems appropriate (generally volunteers should travel in pairs to increase safety and efficacy). There will never be a charge for Warm Line services. And no one will be telephoned or visited who requests not to be.

Warm Line volunteers will be calling just to inquire whether everyone in the household is okay. Every Warm Line volunteer will receive a briefing, before getting started, that will include a request that people's personal problems be treated confidentially. Volunteer mental health professionals, social workers and members of the clergy can help train volunteers to recognize problems and to know how to respond appropriately. Callers will find lots of people who are doing "fine, thank you". But they'll also find physical illness, emotional upsets, relationship crises, financial problems, and even homes needing quick repairs.

Examples: A person with arthritis, living alone, may not be able to open a stuck door; or, an electrical wire may be shorted and arcing dangerously in the home of a person who can't afford an electrician.

Warm Line volunteers will be ready, when it's appropriate, to refer neighbors to free, local support group meetings conducted by Warm Line volunteers. There will be volunteer electricians, plumbers, carpenters, mental health professionals and other skilled people among the volunteers who will be available to help. Sometimes people will be referred to various health care facilities or government agencies, usually when no volunteer individuals or groups are available to deal with the issues. The ultimate goal is to create a community environment in which the latter will never be the case. Of course, paid professionals will be needed for certain severe or on-going problems.

What results do Warm Line volunteers seek? Communities of real warmth and mutual caring — where needed help is readily available. Individuals and families that thrive. Communities where people share feelings, the good and the bad, where supportiveness is the norm and where neighbors are there for neighbors.

This is a social environment we can all live with! And the consequences will impact the physical and mental health of us all. Imagine the impact on law enforcement, health and welfare costs. Imagine the impact on general levels of happiness, satisfaction and fulfillment.

Neighborhood Environmental Committees — Another useful and innovative volunteer group would be the Neighborhood Environmental Committee, ideally to be found in every neighborhood. This group would look after the local, not quite so personal environment, including locally consumed waters, foods and local pollution of air and ground water. Local radon levels can be measured for neighbors in appropriate geographical areas, and houses can be checked for asbestos, lead and other hazardous substances. A more practical job for this committee would be to help clean up dangerous and unsightly trash in the neighborhood.

We can think of the Christmas in April volunteers as a kind of neighborhood environmental improvement group. These thousands of volunteers fix up, paint and repair the homes of the elderly and the indigent every year in many communities across America. A tremendously effective grass-roots organization!

STEPS YOU CAN TAKE NOW

Besides joining, or continuing your activities with existing environmental groups, you can help form the types of committees just described. Chapter 12 deals more with how to accomplish this, but here it can be said that your family, friends and co-workers (or fellow-students) are the best way to start. Another method is to network through Project Jump-Start (see the AFTERWORD).

The most important place for all of us to start is with our own personal environment, within us and without. I recommend making use of a support person or group to help you improve your personal environment. Just establishing a mutually supportive relationship

If I am not for myself, who is for me?

— HILLEL

with even one other person could be the most beneficial step of all.

Another useful step in dealing with your personal environment is to make a written personal environmental inventory. What healthy foods and beverages do you consume? Which ones do you omit? What harmful substances or pollutants do you routinely and knowingly eat, drink and inhale (chemicals and drugs, legal or not, are included)? And what about excessive sun exposure?

I'm not suggesting that you stop taking your prescription drugs. Rather, I'm suggesting that all of us maintain a heightened awareness that questions and challenges ALL swallowed chemicals with "is this good for my internal environment?". Give yourself permission to ask your doctor to justify to you every prescription you take. "Doctor, what will happen to me if I don't take this drug? Are the chances of that happening greater than the odds of severe side effects from the drug?" Remember, your doctor is your hired professional who works for you, not God appearing before you in a white jacket. And while we're at it, are you allowing yourself to be given unnecessary medical tests, treatments and surgeries? Do you need a totally independent second opinion?

When I was in private medical practice, a 42 year old man came in for the third year in a row for a complete physical. It was always at his own request, never at my urging. He was thrilled when the results were normal, but I told him, "I'll trade you these annual physicals, which help me earn a living, for you stopping smoking." He laughed. A few months later this 3-pack a day smoker died suddenly of an apparent heart attack. I didn't want to be proven right. He was a very pleasant fellow. Hey! Listen up! It's not easy, but we all need to take our self-polluting inventories seriously.

Next, your personal survey can deal with your mental and emotional environment. Are you satisfied with your relationships with yourself and others? What ill effects have been caused by, or are likely to stem from, any unsatisfactory and unfulfilling relationships?

Now you can complete your written personal environmental survey by considering the environmental conditions in your home and neighborhood, taking into account physical and emotional conditions and their effects. To avoid the cost of technically trained specialists, which might be needed for total accuracy, you might settle for dealing with things we all know. Are there small children in your home who could get into trouble with dangerous chemicals or drugs within their reach, or for whom you need to fence off a swimming pool? Of course, your vigilant supervision provides the greatest safety factor.

All that's left to do after completing your survey is to take whatever actions you wish, in order to give yourself the results you want. It's your choice whether to work alone or with others.

Do you have at least one support person to contact? Someone who is there for you, come what may? Would you call the Warm Line if one gets organized in your area? Could you talk to a "stranger"? Remember, everyone is a stranger UNTIL we converse. How do you feel about being a Warm Line volunteer, or even an organizer? Would it help if you get to decide how many phone calls you're willing to make? Would five calls a week to people in your area be too many? Do you think you'd get satisfaction from this type of involvement?

When it comes to improving the environment, it's clear that the job is very personal and really does begin with us. It begins with the questions, "How is my personal environment, inside and out? What actions can I take to make the environment better for me, my household, neighborhood and community?"

As the Jewish scholar Hillel said, "If not us, who? And if not now, when?" Shall we begin?

11

RELATIONSHIPS AND FAMILIES THAT THRIVE:
It's Not by Chance

The latest U.S. Census shows that less than 17% of households in big cities are traditional families consisting of a married couple and at least one of their children. With the divorce rate above 50%, with millions of "non-traditional" households, plus the homeless, the traditional family is approaching dinosaur status.

There is a corresponding decline in emotional stability and happiness. Broken homes affect whole communities. Tax dollars are consumed as welfare support for children of deadbeat, absent and alienated fathers. Children raised without fathers as male role models often become seriously troubled youths who, in turn, often trouble the communities around them. Just look at the soaring crime rates among juveniles.

Grass-roots volunteers are definitely involved in repairing the problems associated with troubled and broken relationships. And, while some transformational work is underway, much more is needed.

Of the five Big Issues that I focus on in this book, relationships is the last to be dealt with. But, it's the most important. Why?

Because how we relate to ourselves and others underlies our effectiveness in life — our ability to cope with any and all issues.

RELATIONSHIP PROBLEMS AMERICA FACES

Self-Love and Shared-Love — A divorce, a broken home, a homeless person — all are results of relationship problems. And, so are juvenile delinquency, civil unrest and rioting — crime of all types, emotional illness, suicide, injuries, abortion, substance abuse, many physical ailments, failure to do well in school, dropping out of school and failing to thrive on the job or in a career.

It may seem strange to contend that so many problems are really the result of inadequate relationships. Of course, I'm not saying that relationships are the sole operative factor in every case, only that they do underlie everything we are and do.

Americans, like people of any other country, have only two types of relationship problems: the relationship that each of us has with ourself, and the relationships we have with others.

If you share my outlook that all of us need to have unconditional self-love in order to be happy and effective, to be able fully to share love with others and fully to express our talents and abilities, then the fundamental importance of our self-relationship is obvious.

Components of unconditional self-love are self-acceptance, self-esteem, self-worthiness and self-control (sometimes called "self-mastery").

Check out the self-love levels of addicts and criminals. Low. Now check out the self-love levels of people who belong to, and take responsibility for families that thrive — of people who successfully contribute to their own well-being and that of those around them and their communities. High.

Grass-roots activists, then, have a large stake in being able to assist in enhancing self-love among the people of our communities.

Our "relationships with others" covers a lot of territory. Included are the people in our household, our families, co-workers, fellow students, neighbors and members of our own and other ethnic groups.

How well do we relate to others? Some relationships involve only

It is easier to live through someone else than to become complete yourself.

— BETTY FRIEDAN

association, others friendship, familial love or romantic love. Those of us who do not love and care completely for ourselves will have great difficulty loving and caring for others completely. How can we give, or share what we don't have?

Let's check out the shared-love relationships, friendships and associations of the addict or the criminal. Troubled, unhealthy, even non-existent. Then, let's look at the relationships, friendships and associations of people generally. You find mixed results. People with successful careers often have at least some good working relationships, but may not have long-lasting marriages, or good loving relationships with their children, parents and siblings.

Besides the effects on the children, breakdowns in marriages can lead to financial difficulty, emotional stress that can cause depression, physical illness, or both. These, in turn, can result in joblessness, substance abuse and homelessness.

Clearly grass-roots activists interested in community-betterment have a large stake in assisting people to have strong marriages and other types of good interpersonal relationships.

The abortion rate, the rate of sexually transmitted diseases such as AIDS, the spread of hepatitis and AIDS by needles, and the prevalence of substance abuse are all correlated with inadequate self-love and shared-love relationships.

Those with poor self-love may allow their insecurities to lead them to have unprotected sex, and the inability to develop a shared-love relationship may lead to a life-style of casual sex and promiscuity. Sometimes the fear of being rejected leads people with low self-esteem into that life-style. Low self-esteem allows "peer pressure" to get many young people into trouble with crime and drugs as well. People with very high self-esteem generally do not fear rejection, and therefore do not feel the need to comply with questionable behavior to gain acceptance.

Let's be honest. We all know that pregnancy is 100% preventable, as is AIDS. An integral part of self-love is self-control. It's easy to joke about these matters. Humor is frequently used to hide our embarrassment, such as over NOT being in control of our own lives. Our insecurities breed defensiveness, which robs us of the self-control we need in order to get the results we really want for our lives. But, when we have the self-love we need, then we don't have the insecurity level that undermines self-control.

People <u>with</u> adequate self-love give themselves permission to have negative feelings and to express them to one or more support persons. In this way, substance abuse is not seen as necessary to cover up those negative feelings.

I'm sure that many of us have a great deal of the self-love we need, but few, if any, of us have as much as we could really use. And, while many of us have marvelous relationships with others, few of us can claim that all of our relationships are just the way we want them to be.

Inter-Group Relations — Inter-group relations are of paramount importance to any sizable American community. Our ethnic diversity, certainly a major source of our country's strength, demands that members of each group not only tolerate, but also appreciate all other groups. The results of poor ethnic relations were obvious in the Los Angeles riots of 1992. Similar, though less widespread violent results have been seen on the streets of Brooklyn, Miami and other cities.

If our main, though false, sense of identity and security is based on being a member of an ethnic or other group, rather than primarily on being an individual, then we can enhance that false sense of security by berating, hating and denigrating members of other ethnic groups. Yes, it's as sick as it reads, but it's very prevalent in America and the world.

This mentality says, "If I can look down on you and your group, then I can feel that I and my group are superior."

This outlook perpetuates job and housing discrimination, opportunity denial, criminal behavior and rioting, not to mention distrust and severe limitations on whom we can relate to, learn from and grow with. We limit our opportunities and possibilities to appreciate others, and therefore to appreciate ourselves.

So, grass-roots activists have their work cut out for them in the area of promoting good relations between individuals of all ethnic groups.

Yet, with all our relationship problems, America has relation-

153

There can be hope only for a society which acts as one big family, and not as many separate ones.

— ANWAR AL-SADAT

ships and families that thrive, and communities too. It's never by chance. In every case, you'll find people with sufficient self-love to be able to share love and to take responsibility for all their relationships with others.

HOW GRASS-ROOTS WORK IS HELPING RELATIONSHIPS

Religious groups are particularly active in promoting successful family life. Example: The Mormons have a program called "Home and Visiting Teaching", in which neighbors telephone and visit each other monthly. The program is intended to nip problems in the bud, and is close to the Warm Line proposal of Chapter 10. Most religions stress the importance of strong families that enjoy closeness and love. And, most encourage good interfaith relationships and attempt to fight prejudice.

Support groups exist in some communities, both religion-sponsored and non-denominational. But, we know these efforts are not enough. Too many relationships still fail to thrive. About half of all marriages end in divorce in our big cities.

TODAY'S "HELP" FOR RELATIONSHIPS FALLS SHORT

Many private seminars, and psychotherapy, are available to assist with relationships, but are often very expensive and not so often successful.

Frequently, only one member of a troubled marriage goes for therapy, and that person is usually given full support and encouraged to feel "right", while the absent marital partner is made "wrong". The result of this "therapy" is divorce. Some talk-radio therapists are so extreme in encouraging every caller to quit their relationships, that they could be nick-named "Dr. Divorce" or "Dr. Break-Up".

Today, relationships suffer from false assumptions, ideas that are not effectively countered by "therapy". Somehow we've come to believe that in any dispute one party must be right and the other wrong. When bad results occur, someone has to be at fault, someone has to be blamed and, if possible, punished. So in any troubled (FAULTering) relationship, each party seeks to prove that he or she is the angel, which means, of course, that the other is the devil. When we talk with one member of a broken relationship we always seem to be talking to the angel — until we meet with the other member.

The second false assumption is that fifty-fifty relationships are ideal. The expression "fifty-fifty" dates back only to 1913. In recent decades the term has increasingly been applied to personal, not just business, relationships. The idea is that the responsibility for a relationship ought to be shared fifty-fifty by the couple. The assumption is that when a relationship fails, it's because one partner hasn't shouldered their half. Our increasing divorce rate, and relationship difficulties, have been greatly worsened by this fifty-fifty misconception.

What's the truth, if the assumptions of right versus wrong (angel/devil) and 50/50 responsibility, are false? Let's face it. Relationships thrive only when each person takes FULL, 100% responsibility for his or her relationship. When one person lets down, or is unable to give full support to the relationship, the other partner must carry the full load for the time being. The roles will switch soon enough! And, quarrels over who is "right" or "wrong" in a relationship usually involve power struggles in which insecurities and defensiveness arise. When couples help each other to be more secure, with a timely "I love you" and other forms of supportiveness, the quarrel's over. And no one has to be right.

Given today's high divorce rate, poor inter-group and other relationship problems, what can WE do by our grass-roots activism to turn America's relationship problem around?

INNOVATIVE ACTIVITIES NEEDED NOW

Already grass-roots activists have formed support groups of many kinds, not only for those who are ill, but for the families and close friends of the victims of diseases.

Warm Line volunteers can certainly help form support groups for people with relationship problems, and these can include parent-child relationships and others, not just romantic ones. Besides Warm Line groups, anyone can network to start a support group. It may be

*Personal relations
are the important thing
for ever and ever...*

— E. M. FORSTER

*Constant togetherness is fine —
but only for Siamese twins.*

— VICTORIA BILLINGS

Reprinted by permission of ED STEIN

helpful to have a mental health professional involved as a volunteer, but being of support to others is something most people can do.

I hope you share my beliefs that: (1) People are generally trainable, and they would like to know how to have better relationships; and (2) enough is known about healthy and mutually supportive relationships to make grass-roots efforts, on this critical issue, feasible and worthwhile.

Free support groups can help a lot of people who can't afford professional help, or who aren't willing to pay for it. And these support groups may even produce better results. We have to recognize that many people, especially men, resist going to mental health professionals for relationship problems. Perhaps they'll be more likely to attend support group meetings in which everyone present, including themselves, is there to give support, not just to receive it.

What results are we seeking? Everyone who attends can be committed to helping themselves and others to have better, stronger and more fulfilling relationships. Even those who identify themselves as group leaders can be benefited in their own relationships by the sessions. Support is good for everyone. Family, romantic and even inter-group relations can be handled by volunteer support groups.

Whoever helps lead a relationship support group will hopefully put the kibosh on the fifty-fifty notion and on the right-versus-wrong concept.

Support groups can also help us with our relationships with ourselves. We all need self-love sufficiently strong to fight off emotional insecurities. Why? Because those insecurities make us fight to look "right", even if we have to make someone we love "wrong". And to the extent we are insecure, our ability to love and appreciate others, and to express our talents, will be impaired.

Schools, especially non-governmental, community-owned and operated schools, could provide excellent training for stronger self-relationships, and family and inter-group ties. Only widespread grass-roots involvement by people who care, and who get into action, can accomplish this.

ACTIONS YOU CAN TAKE NOW

Where do we start? The first place all of us can start, regardless of the issue, is with ourselves. How is our own self-love level? Perhaps we can use some support from ourselves and others to improve it. Can we, as adults, be our own supportive "parents" to boost our emotional strength?

A little networking can easily get a support group going. It can be done within a household or family. It can be done with co-workers, through religious or other groups and clubs, or by neighbors. Meetings can be held in someone's home, a school room in the evening, outdoors in a park or around a cafe table.

Good support groups boost the goals and aspirations of all who attend. "Bagging" on each other should not be tolerated. If anyone has something supportive to say, fine. Otherwise, listening is recommended. Attentive and empathetic listening, by the way, is a very effective way to be supportive of others. Criticism can always be transformed into positive suggestions, "Have you ever thought of talking things over before pounding on the walls?" Most people seem to get more support from questions — "So what are you going to do about it?" or "What's your next step and when do you plan to take it?" — rather than direct advice.

Would you like to be a support group leader? Or, you could help with the networking and organizing to get a group started. Do you know someone who would make a great support group leader, or people who could really benefit from the group?

Does your local school have any program or class to raise the self-love (I don't mean self-centeredness) levels of the students? If not, you could be the one who gets that program going. It may be easier to call it a class or program to raise "self-esteem", because, while "self-love" is the more general term that includes self-esteem, people aren't familiar with it. It may also be better to describe what you're advocating as a "class" or "program", because "support group" is also a less familiar term, especially for a school activity.

Before long, in such a student group, defensiveness and insecurity will decline as self-love levels rise. Then, conversations about relating with each other — including members of other ethnic groups,

160

and with family members, become possible and fruitful.

Imagine the homes, neighborhoods and communities we will have when we all relate securely with ourselves and we are able to be fully responsible for all of our relationships!

12

GRASS-ROOTS GAME PLAN:
Organizing for Results

Nearly a hundred million Americans are involved in grass-roots volunteerism. This explosion of activity is just the beginning of America's grass-roots revolution.

Our problems persist not because too few people are involved, although more volunteer work by more people would help. Our problems persist because most of our grass-roots efforts have been reparative, not transformational.

For America to be truly jump-started, this revolution must now enter a new phase in which innovative activism will produce transformational results regarding education, crime and drugs, health care, our personal environment and our relationships. To qualify as a "jump-start", the results we at the grass roots are going to produce must be remarkable and must be achieved within a very few years. Any lesser outcome is likely to encourage apathy, cynicism, and a further downward slide of our society.

New grass-roots strategies, such as those presented in the preceding five chapters, aim at altering the personal and social framework in which problems occur. We can create new systems and conditions that promote good results and prevent problems, rather than spend all of our energies picking up the pieces left by existing systems and conditions that work poorly.

New and expanded possibilities for Americans of all ages to experience joy and fulfillment on a daily basis, is the transformational result we seek. This joy and fulfillment will come from the very process of producing results with regard to the Big Issues, as well as from the results themselves.

But how can we get Community Schools started? Or Community Health Association Plans? Or Regulated Drug Access for Addicts? Or Project Miracle youth activities? Or networks of Warm Line volunteers? Or Relationship Support Groups in our neighborhoods? Or any other innovative solutions that we, the jump-starters of America, wish to implement?

If you're ready and willing to be "part of the solution", let's look at how you can best organize yourself and your community for successful grass-roots action.

All of us who want to be effective are in the same boat. We all need a grass-roots game plan — a modus operandi we can use to get the results we want.

GETTING YOUR GAME PLAN GOING

Defining your role — If you're an activist, or willing to be one, then you're especially interested in knowing how best to organize yourself and your community for successful grass-roots action. You may already be a good organizer.

An activist is simply a volunteer who takes action with sufficient vigor and assertiveness to get the desired result. Activists don't just march in a demonstration, they organize it. They don't just write a letter to their elected representative, they organize and take responsibility for the whole letter-writing campaign.

And every activist needs a cadre of fellow-activists and volunteers for any sizable project to be successful. So if you're more comfortable helping out once someone ELSE gets a good community project going, you can still be tremendously helpful and effective as a volunteer. Some people straddle the line between being an activist or a volunteer. Example: Someone else started the group, but you become the organizer's right-hand person.

Choosing A Specific Goal — Chapter 3 began our discussion about choosing issues and getting started. We tend to be most passionate about issues that have affected us directly, or someone we care about. We know we need to choose our most important issue, or no more than two, because we don't want to spread ourselves too thin to be effective. Once we know what issue we want to work on, we need to define a specific goal or result.

Let's "walk through" getting a game plan going. Suppose education is your main issue. As one example of Thinking Big, as you should, you want better educational results all over the country. Great. But what do you mean by "better"? Let's be specific. You answer that you're referring to improved math and reading comprehension scores on standardized tests. Fine, but how much improved? You decide that your goal is a 20% average total improvement to be accomplished over the next five years. You can use this Q & A technique to arrive at your specific goal for any issue. Now, to get started, you'll need to shift from Thinking Big to Starting Small. What will your first step be?

Evaluating — The first step is to gather local information and evaluate it. What are the current test results at a school near you (or substitute the local aspects of any other specific issue). If you have a child in elementary school, how can you get your own child's scores up? What is the school's present educational environment? Are the teachers and teaching methods adequate? You may need to interview parents, the principal, teachers and students. Are teacher's assistants needed in the classrooms? Are the textbooks good enough? Does the school's principal set a good tone for education? Now analyze your own child's school work, or that of the children of friends of yours who share your goal. What problems do you see? What community organizations are already active, in your neighborhood or community, that share your goal? Are you able to locate a group or any of its activist-leaders that are trying to accomplish a result that you favor?

Getting Support — Once you've chosen a goal, you'll find it helpful to find at least one person who is willing to encourage you, to listen to you with empathy when you run into obstacles and to cheer for you when you've made some progress. If you're lucky, you'll find a committee or organization already working toward your goal. Then, all you need to do is join in, and choose a specific area in which you can contribute your energy and ability.

Avoid or ignore negative support at all costs. You may find that there are always people around who believe that discouraging you is for your own good. Apparently, you need to be saved from yourself. These people may love and care for you, but they're not boosting your chances for accomplishment that will add joy and fulfillment to your life. Please do whatever it takes to find at least one person you can count on for positive support. You'll be glad you did.

Networking and Recruiting — This means getting in touch with organizations and individuals who share your goal. There are many ways to find them. You can ask at your local school, or inquire from the school board. Large public and university libraries often have directories of local and national volunteer organizations (see Chapter 3). Newspapers, and radio and television stations in your area may have in-house libraries that can help. Discuss your issue with family, friends, neighbors and co-workers (or fellow students). You'll quickly find out who's interested in your goal and who isn't. You can use Project Jump-Start (see the Afterword) to assist you in networking. You'll need to decide whether to join an existing group, alone or with people you've recruited, or to form your own committee. Even a small committee can grow into a large organization. Most, if not all, nationwide groups started as small, local committees.

What's the secret of recruiting? No secret. Just common sense. Don't waste time recruiting anyone who doesn't share your vision. But, when you've found a friend, relative, co-worker, fellow-student or anyone else who does, honestly commend them for their enlightened viewpoint, and sincerely invite them to do one thing with you that deals with your goal. The "one thing" could be attending a meeting, helping you with an interview, or assisting you in getting out a mailing. Usually, people are very impressed when they see

If one advances confidently in the direction of his dreams, and endeavors to live the life which he has imagined, he will meet with a success unexpected in common hours.

— HENRY DAVID THOREAU

themselves effectively in action. Give your "recruit" as much credit and power as you can, and you'll probably see that person quickly become as involved as you are.

Planning — There's a lot to plan. What are the first steps for you and your group to do? How many people do you need? If you succeed locally, will you expand? How will you network with people in other areas? Do you want publicity? Will you contact local media? Will you prepare stories to send them about your activities? Maybe you know someone in public relations who will help you with publicity to make attracting people to your cause easier.

Taking Action — Someone has to carry out each step of your group's plan. The group needs to choose leaders or committee chairpeople to carry out the various steps. And, the steps need to be coordinated, with regular feedback to the whole group. That feedback is almost certain to result in new planning and new steps. How often should your group meet, and where? You'll need to decide how much can be done by telephone and at what points you need in-person meetings.

Delegating — Sometimes it's tempting for us to be a one-person show. It goes like this, "I'll just do it all myself. That way I know it'll be done right." Don't fall for it. It's a trap. Your project has a much better chance to achieve great success if you can involve more people. Let them all play roles, and encourage them to take those roles seriously and to give themselves credit for what they do. Yes. Give away credit and power every day, and YOUR success will grow.

Acknowledging — People need to know they're appreciated. And they deserve it. You can help organize special moments of recognition at meetings, even plan award luncheons or dinners as your group grows. These events can sometimes double as fund-raisers. Your event will be a bigger hit if you can get at least one celebrity involved, or any locally prominent person. Find a reason to give an award, a plaque or certificate, to that person for being part of your cause. Not only will that encourage your prominent guest to come, it will gain publicity for your cause and greater attendance for your event. You will get well-deserved acknowledgment if you keep your speeches, and everyone else's, short.

KEEP YOUR EYE ON THE DOUGHNUT

Staying Focused — When I was in medical school in Berkeley, California a long time ago, there was a doughnut shop near campus with a motto on the wall that went something like this, "As through life, my friend, you go, keep your eye upon the doughnut, and not upon the hole."

Not only do we need the emotional strength not to quit when the going gets tough, we also need to keep focused. It's all too easy to get caught up in the personal bickering, jealousies, power struggles and petty politics that seem to go with being human and being part of any group.

What's the answer? There probably is no perfect one. But, staying focused will always help. You're focused if, through thick and thin, you remember that what you want is the RESULTS, and you let nothing get you off track. You're after a particular kind of community-betterment. That's why you're involved. You suspect, and perhaps you've already experienced, that real joy and fulfillment flow from being involved in a worthy cause — from seeing your dream of community-betterment brought into reality and in knowing that you were part of the process.

Giving Away Power and Credit — How far are YOU willing to go to experience that joy and fulfillment? Surely it's worth giving power away to others and giving them credit on a daily basis.

Paradoxically, the more you give away power and credit, the more power and credit seem to come to you. The more you doubt that outcome, the more you should try it, because you have a pleasant surprise in store.

For example, when it comes to giving away credit: You publicly say that John and Nancy were invaluable in obtaining great results by having sold more tickets to the fund-raiser than anyone else. Nancy responds by saying that you made their sales job far easier by

It is amazing how much can be accomplished if no one cares who gets the credit.

— JOHN WOODEN

arranging for wonderful prizes to be offered using the ticket stubs in a raffle at the event. Try as you will, you can't seem to give away more than you get.

It works the same way with giving away power. What I'm saying is, let others have their way. If their way works, you were part of their solution and you have results. If doing things their way doesn't produce results, they may try it your way next. You could become known for your quiet, non-pushy wisdom. And think of the possibly destructive bickering you avoided.

OVERCOMING OBSTACLES

You're on your way. You've got your game plan going. But, let's talk about what you're up against, the obstacles you're likely to face — and ways of preventing or overcoming them.

Us — Walt Kelly said it best in his *Pogo* comic strip, "We have met the enemy, and he is us." Yes, we are our own greatest, and most consistent obstacle. When we look back at the times when we didn't get the results we wanted, wasn't the most common reason because we quit before the results were obtained? Some roadblock, something that stopped us at the moment, became our signal (reason, excuse) to quit.

And how do we know when we've quit? We've quit when we can't name our next step and say when we plan to take it.

It's common to blame others when we don't succeed in reaching our goals. They are at fault, or perhaps it's the system. Sometimes we blame ourselves, which is so depressing it may keep us from being able to clean up old messes or accomplish new things. None of these blaming tactics get us the results we want.

Why not just take full responsibility for our lives, and forget about blame and fault? Why not define ourselves in terms of what we care about and are committed to, and then just get into action NOW to achieve our goals? Why not keep going regardless of the roadblocks, barriers, detours and problems we encounter — by quickly naming our next step and saying when we will take it?

We CAN succeed in not being our own obstacle, but there are

171

still others to overcome.

People — Yes, people will say they're interested, then flake on you. They may show up only when it's time to take credit for whatever is accomplished. Others will try to take control.

The solution? It helps to remember that when people spend their energy trying to look good, rather than be good or do good, it's due to their insecurities. The more secure you can make them feel, the more cooperative and productive they will become. So share power and always give credit to others. Results will follow.

Regulations — There is a law, fee, permit, penalty or tax affecting just about everything you want to accomplish. It may help to have an attorney be part of your volunteer team. Defying unfair regulations and going to jail helped Martin Luther King, Jr's quest for civil rights. Fortunately, most of us will neither want, or need, to go that far.

Money — I'm no expert when it comes to fund-raising. Maybe you are, or you know someone who is. One thing I do know — you rarely get any money unless you ask for it. You can apply to charitable foundations for grants (try using the *National Directory of Non-Profit Organizations*, or *Charitable Organizations of the United States* at your local library to help you find a suitable grantor), or to government agencies. My personal preference is to leave the government bureaucracy out of the picture if you have a choice. For large sums of money, it's worth forming a non-profit charitable foundation.

If smaller sums will do, bake sales, 10K runs, and auctions of donated goods, services and trips may be successful whether or not the money is tax deductible to your donors. Sometimes a letter to everyone you know, with a request that each of them send a copy of your letter with their own note to ten people they know (that's right, a charitable chain letter), may work well. Printers and stationers have been known to give discounts for excellent causes. And don't forget the possibility of using the post office's bulk mailing rates.

A lack of funds is less likely to keep you from reaching your goal than is a lack of undying enthusiasm. A high energy approach may

...victory finds a hundred fathers but defeat is an orphan.

— GALEAZZO CIANO

do you more good than a big budget.

Time — Let's say you're committed to a particular issue. But you still need to work full time for a living, and you have family and other commitments. Somehow you manage to squeeze in two to four hours a week for your volunteer efforts. So far so good, but what happens when you see that more time is needed, time you can't afford?

Networking and delegating may be the answer. Getting the results you want shouldn't cost you your personal relationships, marriage or ability to earn a living. Even retired folks need to balance their commitments (what about the grandchildren?) and avoid physical exhaustion. You may need to recruit more people. Remember. You're doing them a favor when you invite them to join in activities that will help fulfill their lives.

Burnout — This is what happens when we become people pleasers, when we fail to say "no", and end up working harder and longer than we really want to. We know burnout has hit us when we begin to hate the same activism we used to love, or when we abruptly and completely quit.

The best form of prevention is to keep our balance by setting firm limits on our involvement. Good recruiting, networking and delegating can keep our goals on target and help us dodge the burnout bullet.

Frustration — Sometimes our patience wears thin. We want results more quickly than what's actually happening. We may be tempted to quit in order to relieve our frustration. So, what are some constructive ways to get relief?

Try charting the progress you and your group have made on a calendar, a chart or in a diary. When frustration sets in, look at your record of progress and take comfort. It may help to use imagery: Imagine the result you're working toward, and picture yourself descending a staircase, step by step toward that goal. Now imagine your joy as you approach and finally grasp your chosen result. See that result as a reality. How do you like it? Good. Now get back to work — by naming your next step and saying when you'll take it.

WHAT'S IN IT FOR YOU, AND FOR US ALL?

Okay. Let's say you've done it. You followed your grass-roots game plan. You persisted. You overcame obstacles. You got the results you wanted. You got personal satisfaction, too. Maybe even joy and fulfillment.

But what are the general rewards that we all can reap from the kind of grass-roots activism that is both innovative and transformational enough to overcome the Big Issues? Let's talk about those rewards in Part III.

Never give in, never give in, never, never, never, never — in nothing, great or small, or large or petty — never give in except to convictions of honor and good sense.

— WINSTON CHURCHILL

i can't go on...
i really
can't go on
i swear
i can't go on
so
i guess
i'll get up
and go on

— DORY PREVIN

PART III

REWARDS AND DECISIONS
IN OUR HANDS

13

THE PEOPLE
WE BECOME,
THE NATION
WE THEN ARE:
A Possible Dream

Almost one hundred million Americans can't be wrong. That's the estimate of how many of us are already active as grass-roots volunteers.

Nobody's paying us money for our involvement, so we must be motivated by other considerations. Some of us are joy and fulfillment junkies. We go for satisfaction and happiness. Some of us love being part of the solution. We love seeing the results we dream of come into reality, and the peak sweetness is knowing that WE helped make it happen. (Results are even sweeter if we achieve them after we've been told "it can't be done" and "you're wasting your time".)

What kind of people do we become? Our grass-roots involvement transforms our lives into a series of very special and joyful experiences. We become people who expect more of ourselves than of others, and more of ourselves than we ever did before. We learn to work with others cooperatively to get community-betterment results. We learn to appreciate and acknowledge others, which only increases our appreciation of ourselves, and leads to others appreciating us more, too. We're the nearly 100 million people you're not

181

afraid to meet in a dark alley.

This grass-roots revolution is not made up of unhireables with nothing better to do. This is a phenomenon that includes people at every economic level, including employers and employees. It's a movement that's almost 100 million people strong and growing, and represents what an entire nation's people are rapidly becoming.

Voluntary involvement allows people to define themselves in terms of their commitments. It helps us to see that in fact we ARE the sum of our commitments that we honor and live up to.

Some Americans have become famous because of their unyielding and successful commitment to a specific issue or result. Andrew Carnegie, Clara Barton, Jonas Salk, Betty Ford, Ralph Nader and Martin Luther King, Jr., all fit that mold. Yes, they and others became famous, but when asked, such people generally speak of joy and fulfillment as being their reward, not fame.

With so many Americans taking part in the grass-roots revolution, what sort of nation are we likely to become? Without the implementation of transformational innovations, our volunteerism is likely to amount to no more than putting more and more *Band-Aids* on wounds that will keep on expanding faster than we can bandage.

But if even a small percentage of us millions of volunteers turn to innovative programs, we could see a national transformation of epochal proportions. Imagine an America with health care democracy, community-based non-governmental schools, regulated drugs for addicts, Warm Line programs and relationship support groups.

In ten years we could have a much more enjoyable, happier, healthier and safer America. The crime rate and prison population could be cut in half. We could, in that same period, see the end of gang versus law enforcement drug wars in our streets; much lower drug usage; closer and stronger families; much lower divorce rates and rates of unwanted pregnancies — leading to lower abortion rates; younger marriages, starting with 18-year-olds ready to earn a decent living, leading to fewer sexually transmitted diseases and fewer people emotionally disturbed or scarred by repetitively broken, uncommitted relationships.

Having emotionally stronger individuals will lead to greater productivity, better self-care, sounder marriages, stronger and more

182

When great causes are on the move...we learn that we are spirits, not animals, and that something is going on in space and time, and beyond space and time, which, whether we like it or not, spells duty.

— WINSTON CHURCHILL

loving families, lower crime rates and better inter-group relationships. These advances, combined with improved and Accelerated Education and vocational training in our schools, will result in a successful economy for almost everyone. Inner-city or any other poverty will be relatively rare.

Sound pretty good to you? Great. But that's all it is — good-sounding stuff — until WE really get behind innovative grass-roots activities. Without US, none of these results, none of these dreams, will be brought into reality. WITH our committed involvement, all of these results are possible. Yes, these ARE possible dreams we dream.

In the long run men hit only what they aim at.

— HENRY DAVID THOREAU

14

THE EXAMPLES WE SET, THE WORLD WE GET:
A Familiar Story

We set the example for the world with democracy, with our constitution and with our market-driven and profit-motivated economy. Most of the world now tries to emulate America, even surpass us if they can, in these areas.

The result has been a world we can more easily live in, a somewhat less desperate and hostile world. For instance, the end of the Cold War was closely related to people behind the Iron Curtain yearning and struggling for personal and economic freedom. And the establishment of democracies in Latin America in recent years has led to greater freedoms and stability, and to economic advancement in a number of countries.

Setting examples for the world is not about American supremacy, nor a foreign policy of domination. Rather, it is about people worldwide voluntarily emulating us because they see the value of our personal and economic freedoms. In fact, imitating America has become a familiar and frequently repeated story around the world.

Now we're setting the example for the world with our grass-roots revolution. Is there any reason to believe that community-betterment from the bottom up rather than from the top down is uniquely American, a phenomenon that cannot occur anywhere else?

It's true that the activism in other countries that we hear about most tends to involve terrorism and violent civil unrest. But this is a false impression. Lech Walesa led the Polish people, non-violently, away from Communism and Soviet domination as part of a strictly grass-roots movement. Similar movements grew throughout Eastern Europe and in the former Soviet Union itself. In Western Europe, activism for privatization is widespread, and environmental activism is stronger at the grass roots in some countries than it is in America. And look at the marches of tens of thousands of concerned Germans protesting Neo-Nazi violence. So, it's clear that successful grass-roots movements for freedoms and reforms are occurring worldwide.

And, what if WE, in America, DO solve most of our Big Issues? Do you think that people all over the world will know or care about our accomplishments? You bet they will. And do you suppose they'll try to emulate our accomplishments in their own countries? They've copied our successes before, so why not again?

Why do we care whether or not people in other countries solve THEIR Big Issues? For one thing, they'll be more self-sufficient, requiring less help from us. Also, they'll be less likely to go to war with their neighbors because of internal problems, and you know how easy it is for America to get caught up in wars. So the world will be a friendlier and more peaceful place in which to live.

Another plus for us Americans is that when other countries are doing well, there is less incentive for new waves of immigrants to come here. Who would want to leave their native land, families, friends and possessions behind unless conditions are terrible or dangerous? Reduced immigration will give us some breathing room for our economy to accommodate those who have already come here in recent years.

So, solving OUR Big Issues can be expected to have worldwide benefits that will include us. It will pay off handsomely for us to set an example once again for the world. Sure, the Big Issues in other countries may be somewhat different than ours. But, the principle of innovative solutions being implemented at the grass roots is the same everywhere.

The Example We Set, The World We Get

Yes, the examples we set do help determine the world we get. The effects can be positive, significant and very rewarding. Now it's up to us to set those examples.

15

DECISION TIME:
What Part Will You Play?

You've got some decisions to make.

Your own dreams will make those decisions for you, if you let them. What decisions? What dreams?

Decisions: Do you become a grass-roots activist to help jump-start America? Or, do you simply continue your current volunteer work? If you're not already involved, do you begin? Doing what?

That's where your dreams come in: What results would you like to see in your community? Would you like to see those results become widespread throughout the country?

For example, do you dream of a day when our streets are much safer? When drug-related street crimes, including all the shootings and massive costs of the judicial process, are greatly reduced? How confident are you that you'll see these results in the next several years? If you, and others who could become effective jump-starters, get behind innovative grass-roots solutions, will your chances be greater of seeing those improvements?

You can check out the dreams you may have regarding other issues. And, ask yourself how you feel about being part of the solution.

If you've never been involved in any volunteer activity, whether reparative or innovative, you should know this: People who ARE involved often say that no matter how much they give of themselves, they always feel that they get MORE in return. I admit that this is hard to believe — until you see for yourself. And, you may find it hard to get yourself involved in order to experience this phenomenon, if you're not willing to believe that it will happen for you.

If you're ready for innovative grass-roots activities based on your dreams and goals, keep in mind that the road to success isn't always smooth. Here's something cute I've heard that makes the point about the travails of innovators: "How do you identify pioneers? They're the people with all those arrows stuck into them".

What if you're undecided as to what role you're going to play? What if you're going to think it over? No offense intended, but the harsh reality is that for NOW, you've MADE a decision not to participate. Does this mean you'll never get involved? No. With any luck, you'll get another NOW tomorrow.

But NOW is decision time for America, whether or not WE choose to pay attention. Why? Because, for the first time in our history, immigrants are returning to their native lands, after finding America too crime-ridden. Because "THEY" will never give us the results we want. Because we're afraid of what's becoming of us, of America.

And, so what if we're afraid? Without fear there can be no courage. Without courage there can be no worthwhile action.

Come. Come with me and let's look into the mirror. Let's see where the power to make a difference really lies.

AFTERWORD
Project Jump-Start

Black cable on the negative, red on the positive. You turn the key and that engine ignites! But, what if you don't have the cables to make that connection? No matter how charged up you are, you'll need your networking connections if you intend to help jump-start America.

The toughest networking comes after you've checked out your family, friends, co-workers or fellow students. This is especially so if you still find yourself without enough people to join with you, and you can't find a suitable existing group for you to join.

Project Jump-Start is my way of supplying the connecting cables, of helping grass-roots volunteers to network with each other. You could be living on the same street with someone who wants to accomplish the same result you do, but how would you know?

The Project works two ways. (1) You can register your name, address and telephone number, together with the result(s) you would like to help bring into reality. I suggest you register at least two

193

specific results, because you may find that there are several people ready to network with you to get one result, but not the other. (2) At your request, and with the help of your self-addressed and stamped envelope, the Project will send you the names of people and organizations in your area, or elsewhere if we know of none in your area, that share your goals. You'll also receive the appropriate addresses, telephone numbers — and names of contact people, if available. You may access the Project every few weeks for an update. There is no charge for this service.

Please write legibly, and be clear and specific about the results you want, so that it'll be easy to match you with others.

I can't predict how many people will register with the Project. I hope YOU will. Depending on the response, computerization may be needed to ease accessibility, and people will be needed to enter data and to respond to requests.

You guessed it. Of course I'll be looking for volunteers to help run Project Jump-Start.

While the Project is not a dating service, you talk about single people with common interests meeting! Anything can happen and probably will. Even the original, desired community-betterment result may be achieved.

Which brings me to another possible activity for the Project: A Bulletin Board on a computer network may result. If so, news of meetings and accomplishments can be made available to all callers, and a direct method of networking will be at hand. If fees have to be charged to cover costs, they'll be held to the break-even point.

Imagine how helpful it'll be to know who has started a Community Health Association, so you can find out how they did it. And what mistakes did they make along the way that we can avoid? And where has a community school, or system of community schools, been organized? What about clean syringe and needle exchanges? What group has obtained the cooperation of a legislator who is willing to introduce a version of the Regulated Substances Act? Did they use a letter-writing campaign, or did they get someone elected who already favored the legislation? Has your group started a Warm Line in your neighborhood? How is it working? Do you know of any volunteer-sponsored support groups in your area?

AFTERWORD

To register or to inquire, write to:

Project Jump-Start
Grass-Roots Press
P.O. Box 7609
Branson, Missouri 65615-7609

YOU MAY USE THIS PAGE TO REGISTER OR INQUIRE, <u>FREE</u> <u>OF</u> <u>CHARGE</u>, BY PHOTOCOPYING IT AND FILLING IN THE APPROPRIATE INFORMATION BELOW:

Your Name:_____
Address:_____
City:_____ State:_____ Zip: _____
Your phone number (optional): (____)_____
Hours to call: _____

RESULTS I WOULD LIKE TO HELP MAKE HAPPEN:
1._____
2._____
3._____

Please use check marks to make your wishes clear:

I would like to hear by mail only ☐ or by phone ☐ from other people who want to accomplish the same results in my area only ☐ or in any part of the country ☐.

Please send me the names, addresses, phone numbers, organization names and names of contact people who share my goals in my area only ☐ or in any part of the country ☐ according to information available to you.

Results I (we) have already achieved or that are in the works, including names of our organization, key people, key addresses and phone numbers:

_____
_____
_____
_____
_____

APPENDIX A
Text of Proposed
"Regulated Substances Act"

This is the text of what I propose to be included in legislation that Congress will pass within the next two or three years...only if Americans at the grass roots MAKE it happen:

PURPOSES OF THE REGULATED SUBSTANCES ACT:

(1) To remove the profitability from drug dealing, thereby markedly reducing drug-related crime, gang violence and illegal drug importation. To accomplish these goals by providing a carefully regulated system for regular consumers of illegal drugs to obtain small amounts of such substances for their personal use, at prices low enough to make drug dealing hopelessly unprofitable.

(2) To offer amnesty to former drug dealers who come forward willing to quit permanently all drug dealings, and who turn in all illegal weapons and illegal substances in their possession, so that the numbers of drug dealers can be more rapidly reduced than would

occur just by providing habitual drug users with very low-cost access to illegal drugs; to obtain and destroy large numbers of illegal weapons and to get large quantities of illegal drugs off the street marketplace; to permit former drug dealers to begin living more normal and lawful lives for their own benefit, the benefit of their families and of their communities; to permit amnesty to be granted only in such a manner that no information from amnesty applicants regarding other drug dealers, drug sources or drug users may be offered to, or sought by, personnel authorized to grant amnesty, so that applicants for amnesty may confidently come forward secure that no secondary harm awaits them for so doing. The public is to be made aware of this prohibition against using the amnesty process as a means of identifying other drug law violators. Such an awareness is intended to help insure the safety of all who come forward for amnesty.

(3) To permit licensed physicians to treat users of illegal substances with any legal substance as part of a treatment plan aimed at (a) harm reduction to the drug user and the community; (b) detoxification; (c) gradual drug withdrawal over reasonably necessary periods of time; or (d) drug maintenance when withdrawal is not feasible. To permit physicians and patients to arrive at appropriate and mutually agreed upon treatment plans for substance abuse as is done for other ailments.

(4) To permit licensed physicians to administer illegal substances to patients, under reasonable governmental regulation, for medical conditions where the illegal substance is known, or believed, by the physician to provide results superior to those obtainable with any known legal substance.

JURISDICTION: The Department of Justice and the Drug Enforcement Agency shall continue their jurisdiction over all substances currently held to be illegal under federal law, and shall also have jurisdiction over the administration and enforcement of this Act.

APPENDIX A

PROVISIONS OF THIS ACT:

I. REGULATED DRUG ACCESS FOR HABITUAL USERS OF ILLEGAL SUBSTANCES.

A. ILLEGALITIES. The sale, possession for one's own use, or possession for sale of all currently illegal substances such as heroin, cocaine and marijuana shall continue to be unlawful and punishable according to existing laws and regulations, except as specifically provided in this Act.

B. DISTRIBUTION. The DEA shall supervise the distribution of illegal substances that have been seized by law enforcement agencies, to all duly licensed and FDA approved pharmaceutical manufacturing firms that wish to participate and agree to comply with all provisions of this Act and all pertinent DEA regulations. The DEA shall have sole authority to disqualify any pharmaceutical manufacturing firm that fails to so comply. The participating pharmaceutical manufacturing firms, having received the drug materials under the direction of the DEA at no charge, will package the substances into individual doses averaging very close to average street doses known to prevail according to data known to and provided by the DEA. Dose packets may then be sold by the firms to all duly licensed pharmaceutical distributors that wish to participate and agree to comply with all provisions of this Act and all pertinent DEA regulations. The DEA shall have sole authority to disqualify any pharmaceutical distributor that fails to so comply, and shall provide current lists of authorized distributors to participating pharmaceutical manufacturers.

C. AUTHORIZED POINTS OF REGULATED SALES. The DEA shall approve as authorized points of sale all duly licensed pharmacies that wish to participate and agree to comply with the provisions of this Act and all pertinent DEA regulations. The DEA shall have sole authority to disqualify any pharmacy that fails to so comply, and shall provide current lists of authorized pharmacies to participating distributors.

D. INCENTIVES. Any participating pharmaceutical manufacturers, distributors or pharmacies that suffer a business loss with regard to their participation under the provisions of this Act shall be permitted to take such loss as a direct tax credit against federal income taxes due for the appropriate year or years. Also, all participating firms are to be held harmless (see below) by those permitted to purchase illegal substances, for all liability pertaining to the preparation and sale of the illegal substances as regulated by this Act, except for gross negligence.

E. SALES PRICES. All substance sales prices under this Act shall be fixed as follows: Manufacturer to distributor price shall be $1 per dose, regardless of the particular identity of the substance; distributor to pharmacy price shall be $2 per dose, regardless of the particular identity of the substance; pharmacy to authorized purchaser price shall be $3 per dose, regardless of the particular identity of the substance.

F. ACCOUNTABILITY. Pharmaceutical firms are to report monthly to the DEA all quantities of illegal substances received and/or in inventory, including the name and address of the supplying law enforcement agency, and all quantities of packaged doses sold, including the names and addresses of the approved distributors to which those packets were sold and sent. Distributors are to report monthly to the DEA all quantities of packets of illegal substances in inventory, purchased and received, including the names and addresses of the manufacturers, and all quantities of packets sold and sent to each participating pharmacy, including the names and addresses of the pharmacies. Pharmacies are to report monthly to the DEA all quantities of packets in inventory, purchased and received from each distributor, including the names and addresses of each distributor, and all quantities of packets sold to authorized purchasers including data indicating the identity of each purchaser and the date of each sale. All participating firms agree that DEA agents may check records and inventories during normal business hours without prior notice. In addition, all participating law enforcement agencies agree to supply the DEA with monthly data regarding any shipments of illegal substances to participating pharmaceutical firms, including quantities, shipment dates, and names and addresses of the receiving firms. The DEA shall determine the permissible methods of shipping, including required security precautions for shipments.

G. MANUFACTURER RESPONSIBILITIES. Pharmaceutical firms will be expected to exclude only extremely dangerous contaminants, such as significant levels of strychnine or insecticides, and shall have no responsibility or liability with regard to purity, or potency of dosages per unit of weight. Dosages may be packaged containing from one to six dosages per packet of each illegal substance regulated by this Act. Each dosage is to be kept, so far as is reasonably feasible, at or slightly below known street dosage packets according to data available to the DEA or to sources deemed reliable by the DEA. The desired result is to cause minimum harm to the authorized habitual drug users, while still discouraging street purchases from illegal sources.

H. WARNING LABELS. Every dosage packet shall have the name of the principal drug contained, together with "DANGER" and "POISON" (including skull and crossbones) warnings. The labels shall also include a statement that the substance is illegal, is not recommended for human consumption and can lead to dangerous habituation, dependency, illness or even death. Every packet dispensed by a pharmacist shall be accompanied by a standard DEA-approved brochure recommending that the authorized purchaser enter a drug treatment program, and the names, addresses and telephone numbers of at least two such local program are to be included (unless none or only one are available locally). Warnings against intravenous injection and the sharing of used needles and syringes, and information on smoking rather than injecting narcotics, are to be included. Each packet label is to have a numerical code so that the pharmaceutical firm, although traceable for DEA purposes only, is not identified by name, to avoid the implication that the pharmaceutical firm endorses the use of the substance.

I. AUTHORIZED PURCHASERS. Authorized purchasers must be 21 years of age or older and must affirm, under penalty of perjury, that they have been currently and habitually using the particular substance or substances for which authorization is sought, including at least three usages of each such substance within the prior two weeks. Every applicant for an authorized purchaser card under this Act must attend and view a DEA-authorized educational video (or hear an audio cassette for the legally blind) lasting no less than thirty minutes nor more than ninety minutes. The video is to explain the dangers of the use of the illegal substances regulated under this Act, and to explain the workings of this Act including the illegality of: (1) the resale or purchase of illegal substances other than as permitted under this Act; and (2) the illegality of sharing, even without charge, of any regulated substance, even with another authorized purchaser. The video also is to explain that each authorized purchaser will receive a DEA registration card which must be presented at the time of each purchase of an otherwise illegal substance at an approved participating pharmacy. At the time the DEA card is issued, the authorized purchaser's signature must appear at the bottom of a pre-printed statement which includes the following: (a) an acknowledge-ment of having viewed the required video; (b) a release from liability of the DEA, the U.S. government, all governments of local jurisdic-tion, all approved and participating pharmaceutical firms, distributors and pharmacies; c) a receipt for their temporary or permanent card; d) an affirmation of their prior habitual and qualifying use of the regulated substance(s); (e) an acknowledgement that neither the DEA, the U.S. government, nor any participating firm encourages, endorses or approves the use of any illegal substance by anyone — that on the contrary, abstinence and drug treatment programs are recommended to end dependence on illegal substances; (f) an acknowledgement that the authorized purchaser understands that the DEA cards are issued only to reduce harm to the drug user and to the community, by reducing illegal drug trafficking and related crimes, especially those committed to help afford street drugs; (g) an acknowledgement of receipt of a list of local drug treatment and/or rehabilitation programs that includes a statement that, under this Act, all licensed physicians may treatment drug addiction, using only legal substances. All items "(a)" through "(g)" are to be included on a single form to be provided by the DEA, and each authorized purchaser is to receive a copy of the signed form at the time of signing.

J. AUTHORIZED PURCHASER CARDS. DEA cards issued to authorized purchasers shall show a photographic likeness of the holder, name, date of birth, address and phone numbers (if any), and shall name the illegal substance(s) which the person is authorized to purchase, as well as the starting date and expiration date of the card. The maximum number of illegal substances that may be purchased by any one authorized purchaser shall be two. The names of the substances on the card may be changed only at the time of annual renewal, upon the request by the authorized purchaser, and no substance may be added except at the time of renewal. Cards shall be issued at the end of the mandatory video viewing session (temporary cards need not have a photo, and other photo identification must be presented to pharmacies, such as passport or driver's license, until a permanent card is issued). Video viewing sites shall be provided by the DEA within 50 miles of the residence of the applicant for a card, and at reasonable times within ten days of receipt of a request for a card by any applicant. Video viewing and issuance of cards shall be at no cost to the applicants. Unless invalidated for cause under this Act by the DEA, all cards shall be issued for a period of one year, and may be renewed by the holder by viewing the then current version of the DEA-authorized video (or audio cassette for the legally blind) within 60 days prior to the date of expiration of the card.

K. REGULATION OF CARD USE. Every participating pharmacy shall be provided by the DEA (at no more than a nominal charge) with electronic or telephonic means of verifying that the presented authorized purchaser card is valid and has not been suspended or canceled. The same electronic or telephonic verification system will verify for the pharmacy that the card presented has not been used at ANY participating pharmacy more than three other times within the current seven-day period, not within the prior 24 hours, and not to exceed the weekly number of dosages as follows: Maximum card usage shall be four per week, with no less than 24 hours between uses, for the purchase of no more than 21 doses per week of each of no more than two regulated substances specified on each card. No more than a 3-day supply of a regulated substance may be purchased at any one time. The verification program will handle all computations of usage, so that pharmacy personnel will see only a readout verifying that the card is valid for use at the current purchasing visit, and stating the maximum number of dosages of each substance that may be purchased at that visit. In addition, the authorized purchaser must sign a logbook verifying the purchase, before the pharmacy may hand over any dosage packet(s). The purchase will include an unused disposable needle and syringe if the purchaser so requests and turns in a "dirty" used needle and syringe in exchange, for which the pharmacy may charge a maximum of one dollar. (NOTE: State and local sales taxes may be added to purchase prices under this Act if required by local or state law.) The holder of an authorized purchaser card shall not be required to have a physician's or other health care practitioner's prescription, nor may any prescription be accepted, for any purchase for which the card is required, by any participating pharmacy.

L. CAUSES FOR SUSPENSION OR CANCELLATION OF PURCHASING PRIVILEGES. Presentation of a card more frequently than four times in one week, or after an interval of less than 24 hours between presentations, may, at the discretion of the DEA, lead to invalidation of the card for a six-month suspension period. Presentation of an invalid card or the card of another person, or any second offense, at the discretion of the DEA, can result in a longer period of suspension or even permanent cancellation of any otherwise valid card. Any illegal possession, resale, possession for sale, or sharing of illegal drugs, even those obtained in accord with this Act, are all punishable according to applicable law; in addition, any holder of a qualified purchaser card found to have committed any such acts shall be subject to a six-month suspension of card usage. Any second offense, at the discretion of the DEA can lead to longer suspension or permanent cancellation of card privileges, in addition to other penalties provided by law. The DEA shall have discretion to waive suspensions and cancellations of card privileges, and may suspend or cancel the card privileges of any card holder convicted of any felony committed after issuance of such card.

II. AMNESTY FOR FORMER DRUG DEALERS.

A. ELIGIBILITY FOR AMNESTY. Any person willing to admit to a history of illegal drug dealing for which no arrest has yet been made, shall be eligible for amnesty from arrest and prosecution for that illegal drug dealing as provided for in this Act. Any such eligible person must sign a written amnesty agreement, and that person shall not be arrested or prosecuted, after such signing, for any illegal drug dealing (for which an arrest has not already been made) so long as that person is in full, good faith compliance with the signed amnesty agreement.

B. APPLICATION FOR AMNESTY. Any person seeking amnesty under this Act shall apply for amnesty at any office of the DEA or FBI as follows: (1) All illegal weapons (unloaded), ammunition, and all illegal drug substances in the possession of the applicant are to be brought by the applicant to the office where application is to be made, in closed bags or other containers, and such materials are to be turned over by the applicant to an authorized agent of the DEA or FBI; (2) the applicant is to complete, date and sign the amnesty agreement form, which is also to be signed by an authorized representative of the DEA or FBI office, and a signed copy is there and then to be handed to the applicant.

C. GRANTING OF AMNESTY. Amnesty shall be in full force and effect at the time the application has been duly completed and signed. The former drug dealer is now free to leave the office of the DEA or FBI and, so long as that person remains in full, good faith compliance with the amnesty agreement, the amnesty shall remain in full force and effect.

D. THE AMNESTY AGREEMENT. In the amnesty agreement, the applicants neither admit nor deny any specific illegal acts. However, they state under penalty of perjury that: (1) they have turned in all illegal weapons, illegal ammunition and all illegal drug substances in their possession or under their control; (2) they verify that they will permanently abstain from any future dealing in or with illegal weapons, ammunition or drugs; (3) and they acknowledge that they have neither been asked, nor have they volunteered, any information whatsoever regarding any person or persons known or thought to be involved in using, owning, buying, selling, storing or otherwise distributing illegal weapons, ammunition or drugs. The applicants further acknowledge their understanding that a conviction for any future illegal involvement with drugs, weapons or ammunition will result in a nullification of this amnesty agreement.

APPENDIX A

III. MEDICAL TREATMENT ENABLEMENT.

A. USE OF ILLEGAL DRUGS TO TREAT PATIENTS. Any duly licensed physician may write a prescription on a federal triplicate controlled substances form, for the use of any illegal substance, up to a maximum of six dosage packets per prescription, to treat any ailment other than habituation or addiction to the prescribed substance itself or to any illegal substance. The prescribing physician must have on record a dated and signed written explanation, or memo, identifying the patient, the type of illegal substance to be used, and the medical rationale for using that illegal substance, including the diagnosis of a medical condition sufficiently serious to warrant the use of an illegal substance. The written memo must include a statement by the physician that to the physician's knowledge, no legally available substance is as capable of producing the desired medical benefit for the patient as is the illegal substance. The approximate dosage of illegal substance is to be included in the memo, together with the anticipated duration of such course of treatment. The prescription may be filled at any pharmacy participating under this Act, by the patient personally (showing photographic identification), or by any person claiming to represent the patient provided that such person shows proper photographic identification together with current address and telephone number (if any). No prescription may be used in conjunction with any authorized purchaser card under this Act. The pharmacies' logbooks for dispensed illegal, but regulated, substances must be signed by the persons receiving such substances, and the logbooks must also show the recipients' printed name, address and telephone number. Illegal substances prescribed in conformity with this Act may be administered to the patients prescribed for, by the appropriate medical personnel in any medical office, hospital, other health care facility or home, or may be self-administered under a physician's directions. The persons or facilities responsible for storing and dispensing illegal substances must keep such substances under safely locked conditions until used for the persons intended, or until safely discarded so that no one else may use the substances.

B. MEDICAL TREATMENT OF HABITUAL USERS OF LEGAL

OR ILLEGAL SUBSTANCES. Any duly licensed physician may, with the agreement of any patient who habitually uses legal or illegal substances such that a drug dependency is diagnosed by the physician, devise any treatment program aimed at the alleviation or improvement of the patient's dependency problem. Such physicians may prescribe any legal substances to their patients, including controlled substances, provided that a treatment plan written and signed by the physician appears in the patient's medical record. The treatment plan must include both rationale and goals, and if controlled substances are being prescribed, the treatment plan must be updated at least monthly including patient progress and any change in rationale or goals. The treatment plan must discuss available alternatives not chosen, together with appropriate rationales. To be valid, a treatment rationale must state how the present treatment plan represents an immediate benefit to the patient's health and well-being, or at least how the plan is aimed at future benefit. Any benefits to the patient's family and/or the community may be included. The mere prescribing of controlled substances to habitual drug users without a bona fide, properly devised and written treatment plan shall remain strictly prohibited. Physicians may not charge any fee for prescriptions, nor may a physician's visit be required for the primary purpose of charging a fee for any prescription written under the sanctions of this Act. No physician or any other health professional may write a prescription for the use of any illegal substance as part of the treatment of any drug habituation or dependency.

APPENDIX B
Text of Proposed "Community Health Association Plan"

What Is the Community Health Association (CHA) and What Are Its Purposes?

CHA is a voluntary non-profit public charitable foundation. Its purpose is to make health care: (1) much more economically efficient and to sustain that efficiency over time; (2) accessible to all residents of the USA regardless of ability to pay; (3) qualitatively the best possible in terms of patient outcomes and satisfaction; (4) a most satisfying choice of professional or voluntary involvement so that sufficient numbers of the most qualified people will be attracted to such endeavors; (5) an active concern of all its citizen member/owners whose voluntary involvement will raise the levels of self-care, preventive measures, wellness-promotion and ultimately health itself in communities so that marked savings in health care costs and human suffering, accompanied by enhanced quality of life, will result.

APPENDIX B

How Will Local Chapters be Formed?

Local chapters will be formed by interested volunteers, in each community, consisting of a mix of health care professionals and lay people. Initially, the national leadership will be located in whichever city is the site of the first chapter. That leadership, in cooperation with Project Jump-Start, will assist volunteers from other communities, who make themselves available for networking, to form chapters in their communities. People from every segment of a community, including all those in the health care professions, need to be recruited through networking and publicity to join in the effort to form local CHA's. Private and public meetings, many of them, will be required. Activist leaders will need to be selected from among those willing to serve.

How Much Will CHA Membership Cost?

CHA dues are suggested at $10 per person per year. For the purpose of voting membership, age 18 is the minimum, except for younger heads of households, and dues and status are equal for health care professionals and lay people. The thinking is that all of us, regardless of profession, are patients at one time or another, all of us have our health at stake, and our interests are therefore all equal in health care issues. The dues amount is intentionally low so as to be as inclusive as possible.

How Will CHA Costs Be Kept Down, and How Will Dues Be Spent?

Members of CHA boards of directors, whether local, regional or national, will all be unpaid volunteers who will expect only reimbursement for necessary and reasonable out-of-pocket expenses on behalf of CHA that exceed $10 in any given calendar quarter. Membership dues will remain with local chapters, except for one dollar per person (ten percent of local dues) of which half will be forwarded to the national CHA board headquarters, and half to the appropriate regional board, to cover national and regional administrative costs, such as printing, postage and telephones. It is planned to recruit donated office space, equipment and volunteer clerical work in order to keep administrative expenses extremely low. Local dues will be spent on membership recruitment, office and clerical expenses, initiation of pilot CHAP programs, and health care education at the local level, including preventive measures, wellness-promotion, better self-care, promotion of CHAP health care plan memberships, and other community activities directed at health betterment.

Who Will Be in Charge of CHA?

At each local chapter level, CHA members will elect its board of directors annually. Every paid-up member will have one vote, and any such member may nominate himself or herself as a candidate for the board. No less than one-third of the members of any local board, nor more than one-half, shall be health care professionals. During any chapter's first year, its year of formation, the initial organizing volunteers will serve as a self-appointed board, and any such members may "run" for a board seat at the first annual election. Depending on local conditions, the first such election may be scheduled before the end of one year, but in no case later than one year from inception. Inception is defined as the date of an agreement by three or more volunteers to form a local chapter of CHA. Local boards should have from three to nine members, depending on the size of the chapter and the number of volunteers wishing to serve on a board. Each local board will elect its own chairperson annually.

Each local board will elect one regional board member once there are three or more chapters in a region. Regional boundaries will be determined cooperatively between local boards and the national board, but in general a regional board shall consist of no more than twenty local chapters, and should cover a geographical area of some cohesion, such as a single municipality, metropolitan area, county, parish or the like. Members of each regional board shall elect one of themselves as regional board chairperson.

An election of national directors shall take place within two months of the time that at least five regional boards have been formed, and at least five regional board members are available to stand for election as a national director. Any member of a regional board of directors may nominate herself or himself as a candidate for the national board of directors, and every local and regional board member shall be eligible to cast one vote for each of no more than five such candidates. The top five vote-getters nationwide shall constitute the national board of directors of CHA for a one-year term, and the five elected national board directors shall elect one of themselves, promptly, to serve as national chairperson of the board, a position of honor and moral leadership more than one of power.

The duties of CHA's national board of directors will be to provide leadership at the highest level, to settle disputes not resolved at the regional or local board level, to recommend CHA and CHAP program and policy changes from time to time, to negotiate contracts that span multiple regions, and to interact with government agencies and officials with jurisdiction over multiple regions. The national board of directors shall have the power to hire and fire an Executive Director, and any other administrative staff deemed necessary due to the lack of sufficient volunteers.

What Will CHA's Activities Be?

CHA's activities will be those activities required, and permitted by applicable laws, to bring into reality the five purposes of CHA as stated above. Such activities will include: (1) the establishment of at least two local pilot health care programs as described below; (2) assuming the pilot programs are operating successfully for at least six months, the establishment, throughout the USA, of similar and permanent programs of health care to be known as the Community Health Association Plan (CHAP), to be made available to every person residing in the USA who joins CHA and who wishes to subscribe to CHAP; (3) the sponsorship and management of educational and inspirational programs, operated by volunteers, aimed at CHA's members and the community at large, intended to foster universal membership throughout the country, better self-care, disease prevention and wellness-promotion; and (4) the participation in lobbying, political candidate selection and election campaign activities, all to support the betterment of community health by such means as the implementing of traffic and other neighborhood safety measures, the lessening of crime and substance abuse problems, and the promoting of health research.

What Is the Community Health Association Plan (CHAP)?

CHAP is a health care plan, based on additional membership fees, offered by CHA to its members only. It is not health insurance. No CHA member is required to join CHAP or pay its fees. It is anticipated that very nearly every CHA member will want to join, however. CHA boards of directors will govern CHAP, with regular input from peer representatives of health care professionals and facilities.

CHA boards will contract with administrators chosen by the boards to administer the CHAP program. No board member shall be affiliated with nor have any ownership interest in any administrative entity contracted with by any CHA board beyond the two-year anniversary of the inception of any such contract. After such date, board members must either resign from board membership or give up any affiliation or ownership interest in any administrative entity having a CHAP contract.

This provision allows initial incentive to get CHAP programs going throughout the country, even when only small numbers of people may be actively involved — but later, after the first two years, when CHAP enrollment and participation will have grown, it is important to have arms-length relationships between boards and the entities with which the boards bargain and contract.

How Much Will CHAP Cost?

CHAP's cost per person is expected to be one-fourth the cost of current private health insurance plans, or even less, after the first two to three years of operation. Costs may be higher during those first two to three years.

CHAP would be the preferred medical plan for private and government employer health programs, because of its efficiencies and its freedom to work with most existing health care providers.

The cost of catastrophic illness (see further discussion below) will require insurance and other measures.

It is expected that the average monthly cost per adult will be $40 or less, $20 per child less than age 13, $30 per teenager, or not more than $100 per month per household consisting of two adults and one child. For many subscribers, some or all of these costs will be paid by employers. CHAP fees will be proposed by CHAP administrators and must be approved by local and regional CHA boards each year, with more frequent changes in fee levels if warranted.

How Will Health Care Cost Savings Be Achieved?

Major cost reductions will be made possible because of the efficiencies and policies of CHAP, and because of the savings produced by the community efforts of CHA, as follows:

(1) Every CHA chapter will be actively involved in educating its membership and the community at large in better self-care, disease prevention and wellness-promotion. Every member household will be contacted by CHA trained volunteers, on a monthly basis, to inquire as to their well-being. Real and helpful volunteer and professional assistance will be made available to members where it is needed and welcome. Every chapter will hold monthly meetings on timely health-related topics, with appropriate health care experts in attendance.

(2) CHAP members will be made very aware of the connection between their own self-care, disease prevention and wellness-promotion activities on the one hand, and their health and the costs of their CHAP fees on the other hand. Every CHAP member, then, will play a role in determining the cost of the next year's CHAP fees, based on the costs of providing health care in the CHAP program.

(3) CHAP members covered by Medicare, Medicaid, Champus or other government-sponsored health care coverages will continue such coverages (and their CHAP fees will be waived), thus reducing the costs of health care to CHAP. (CHA may seek to substitute CHAP coverage for government coverages, but legislation would be required, it isn't known when this might occur, and the method of phasing in CHAP coverage is unknown; the goal would be to have

no overall impact on CHAP costs based on a gradual phase in period accompanied by continuing cost economies across the entire population.)

(4) Membership in CHAP will be enhanced by the fact that many health care professionals, and facilities such as hospitals, will limit their care to CHAP members after a six-month transition period, except for the immediate and stabilizing treatment of the life-threatening emergencies of non-members.

(5) Local fund-raising events will provide fee-payment assistance to the truly needy in each local chapter's area, and local governments may decide to contribute to these fund-raisers, as might United Way and similar charitable organizations. The greater the membership in CHA and CHAP in any local community, the more money will be available for health care costs. The higher the anticipated level of health based on better self-care and more appropriate professional care, the lower those costs are likely to be per person.

(6) Health care professionals and facilities with a record of excessive cases of negligent medical care (including excessive payouts of malpractice awards and settlements), as determined by local CHA boards, will not be eligible to participate in CHAP, thus reducing the risk of negligent medical care for CHAP members and reducing the costs in both suffering and dollars required to pay for such negligence.

(7) Efficiencies in the provision of health care will include approved standards of care, including indications for various surgeries, tests, procedures and lengths of hospital stay barring unusual circumstances, and rapid referral to appropriate specialists and sub-specialists when indicated. No office visits, tests, procedures or operations will be covered by CHAP for the primary purpose of increasing revenues to a health care professional or facility, or for the primary purpose of avoiding liability for possible malpractice.

(8) Further economy will result from elimination of all malpractice insurance premiums, based on the mediation and arbitration of all medical malpractice claims made by CHAP members against CHAP health care professionals or facilities. The arbitrations, to be both compulsory and binding, are to be conducted by local CHA boards who will appoint panels of three arbitrators to hear each such

case. All arbitrators must be CHA member/volunteers, and must include one attorney and one health care professional (either or both can be retired), and one lay member who is a member of the local chapter's CHA board. The arbitrators will first act as mediators, and if mediation proves fruitless after no more than three meetings with the parties, arbitration proceedings will be scheduled for prompt disposition.

The costs of arbitration are known to be much less than those of litigation in court, and are further reduced in this case because the arbitrators are all to be unpaid volunteers. The complaining CHAP member may retain legal counsel, as may the defending health care professionals or facilities. There will be no arbitrary cap on award amounts, but no punitive or exemplary damages will be permitted. However, the arbitrators will have the authority to direct the probation or suspension of the health care professional or facility for one year, or the permanent expulsion when they deem it appropriate and when such is confirmed by a two-thirds vote of the local CHA board after appropriate hearing, from further CHAP professional participation.

It is anticipated that on the whole, awarded damages will be much lower than the highest amounts awarded in jury trials, and that the number of complaints will be much lower than currently found in today's malpractice milieu. Many cases of alleged malpractice will be settled at the mediation level. The prompt resolution of claims by arbitration (generally six months or less versus three to five years in court) will be a boon to the complaining members and to those accused of malpractice, and will be welcome relief to our overcrowded courts.

CHAP professional peer representatives will conduct active continuing programs to help reduce medical negligence and negligence claims. CHAP will pay the amount of all damages awarded, and most, if not all, of the funds to be used for this purpose will come from annual CHAP professional dues paid by health care professionals and facilities. CHAP will have the authority to re-insure itself against malpractice claims made against the program's participating health care professionals and facilities, and would likely do so with an appropriately high deductible (for example, the deductible amount could equal 80% of the total of all annual CHAP professional dues collected).

(9) Economic efficiency will also be achieved by the fact that health care professionals and facilities will have a rapid and progressive diminution to nearly zero of costs for collections and billings. All billings will be to CHAP by a credit card type of voucher process, and since all fees for services will be governed by peer and board-approved guidelines, rarely will disputes or letter-writing be required to collect fees. Patient members are never billed directly, except for their CHAP fees not paid by employers or other sources, and need only to sign their verification that they have received the services being billed for. Payment in full, per approved CHAP fee guidelines, will be deposited to the accounts of the billing providers within two weeks of CHAP receiving proper billing vouchers.

(10) Random auditing combined with sampling audit procedures will guard CHAP against fraud. Any pattern of over-billing will lead to probation, suspension or expulsion, upon vote of the local board, and possible legal consequences to the offender. Regional boards and the national board may also impose probation, suspension or revocation of professional participation privileges, or may overturn rulings by local boards on appeal.

Standards for proper utilization of health care by CHAP subscribers will be adopted by local boards and the national board of CHA, after considering recommended treatment plans and standards of care proposed by health care professional and facilities representatives elected by their peers, and after receiving input from recognized associations of health care professionals. Patterns of improper over-utilization by patients or excessive provision of unnecessary services will both be subject to audit and appropriate consequences by local boards. For example, patients who persist in over-utilization of health care services can be issued cards requiring pre-authorization of all services except for emergency care. Health care providers who provide excessive services will be subject to probation, suspension or expulsion by the proceedings of CHA boards.

(11) Economic efficiency will be further assured by the intelligent sharing of space, equipment and personnel by health care profession-

als and facilities participating in CHAP, and by mandated adherence to CHA approved standards of care.

Sharing of facilities and equipment is a critical part of cost reduction. A building with forty offices need not have forty waiting rooms and forty or more receptionists. There need not be forty electrocardiograph machines with forty trained technicians in the same building. A building with 100 offices need not have 100 or more separate computer systems with 100 or more computer operators. Peer representatives will have to work with their peer professionals and with building landlords to make space-sharing and space utilization more efficient. Some large group medical or dental practices, whether HMO's or otherwise, already have in place many efficiencies involving sharing of resources.

Health care professional members, whether in solo, group, HMO or any other type of practice, and whether physicians, dentists, psychologists, pharmacists, chiropractors, nurses, physical therapists, hospitals, hospices, nursing homes, etc., will each elect peer representatives for each professional category within each local board area. These peer representatives will recommend guidelines for sharing equipment and facilities, and guidelines for standards of care, including treatment plans covering hospital utilization, surgeries, medications, diagnostic and treatment procedures, testing, etc. A further task for peer representatives will be to set standards for fees for various services. All recommendations require CHA board approval. All peer representatives will serve as unpaid volunteers, assisted by appropriately trained lay volunteers and CHA-paid staff as needed. Peer representative duties will include initial evaluation of over- or under-utilization of services by patients or by health care professionals and facilities.

Since net income is obviously more important than gross income, CHAP's economies need not disturb the "bottom line" of those health care facilities and professionals who are not over-providing services. The CHAP goal is to maintain no less than current net profit margins, while markedly reducing costs that inflate gross billings. After allowing for decreases in overhead achieved by sharing arrangements, markedly reduced billing and collecting costs, absence of uncollectibles, absence of malpractice insurance premiums, etc., the gross charges for services should be reduced by 40% from pre-CHAP levels within two years after CHAP is established within any given community.

Will CHAP Members Choose Their Practitioners and Facilities?

Yes. Even HMO's or other closed or restricted panels of practitioners, in order to be eligible to provide care to CHAP members, must permit CHAP to collect all CHAP fees directly from their individual patient members, as for any other CHAP members, and these health care organizations, HMO or otherwise, will bill CHAP administrators as will all other health care professionals.

Within six months of CHAP professional membership, all HMO's and other forms of pre-paid and restricted panel groups will have made a transition to the CHAP system. This will free all of their CHAP member-patients to obtain health care outside the formerly closed or restricted panel. In short, every CHAP member will have free choice of health care professionals and facilities.

Where CHAP involvement in health care is close to universal, CHA members will have a considerable voice over health care delivery, including service, prices, quality, etc. Clearly, CHAP allows all members the widest possible choice of health care practitioners and facilities. The only members who may need to change physicians, when they otherwise don't wish to, will be those whose physicians have chosen not to join CHAP as a health professional member.

Who Will Be Eligible to Serve as CHAP Health Care Practitioners?

Any practitioner or facility legally offering health care services will be eligible to join (contract with) CHAP as health care providers, subject to fulfillment of a few key criteria:

(1) The person, group or facility must have and maintain a good and clean record. There cannot be a record of medical negligence, before or after joining CHAP, as shown by multiple malpractice claims which were either decided, by litigation or arbitration, in favor of the claimants, or resulted in substantial settlements.

Participating medical groups or HMO's must clearly exclude their

219

practitioners with unacceptable malpractice records from participating in the care of CHAP members, prior to the six-month transition period, as each professional in a group is to have individual CHAP clearance for membership.

(2) Professional health care members must be willing to participate in the process of determining local standards of care and fee levels for care within the domain or specialty of services provided by each member. Such participation may only require completing a survey regarding facilities, fees, services and treatment plans.

(3) Professional health care members must be willing to accept the fee levels and standards of care guidelines approved by their peers and the CHA, agree not to bill any CHAP member directly for covered services, and agree to periodic CHAP auditing to confirm compliance with CHAP standards.

(4) Professional health care members must be willing to work cooperatively with peer groups and the board to put into practice the economic efficiencies, discussed above, into their own practices or facilities.

(5) Annual professional membership dues must be paid to CHAP on an annual or quarterly basis, and such fees will be much lower (one-fourth of current costs, or less, is the target) than the malpractice insurance premiums that will no longer be needed after a six-month transition period in each community where CHAP is begun. CHAP administrators will propose professional membership fee levels each year for each category of professional and facility, to be approved by local and regional CHA boards, after consultation with elected professional and facility peer representatives.

What Are the Benefits of CHA and CHAP Participation to Health Care Professionals and Facilities?

(1) Self-determination. CHAP permits health care professionals and facilities to determine their own work context, whether solo practice, group, HMO, etc., whether the same context as before CHAP, or different. The only restriction is that there will be no direct collection of fees from patients for covered services, and there will be no closed or restricted panels after the transition period.

APPENDIX B

Private practitioners can maintain their own practices. Government and insurance companies will not be in full charge as might otherwise occur, and as is already largely true. Standards for care and fees will be set by CHA, but every professional can participate in the process, in which the input of elected professional peer representatives will be given high priority by CHA boards. Note that the boards will have health care professionals as one-third to one-half of its members, and any health care professional may nominate himself or herself as a candidate for the local board, as may any lay member.

(2) Health professionals and their families are patients too, at one time or another, and it will be reassuring for health professionals to know that they are partly the cause, and are an integral part of, a high-quality, low-cost system of health care with complete choice of physicians and other health care professionals and facilities for those who want that choice.

(3) Most health care professionals will be freed from extensive administrative duties and overhead, including billing, collecting and high malpractice premiums, and can concentrate on professional duties. Those health care professionals who are willing to limit their patients to CHAP members only, will be able to cancel malpractice insurance after a six-month transition period.

(4) No longer will there be a sense of impending doom — of health professionals waiting for some grim government ax to fall on them. And they will have the satisfaction of knowing that, along with thousands of lay volunteers, they had a role in solving many of America's health care system problems.

(5) Financial betterment for health care professionals will come from two sources: First of all, peer professional representatives, with local and regional CHA board approval, will establish annual financial reward systems for those professionals and facilities having the best health outcomes. Rewards will typically be in the thousands of dollars, and will be limited only by the success of everyone involved in CHA and CHAP in keeping the system in the black. Regional boards (local boards where regional boards do not yet exist) will annually allocate awards based on peer reviews and patient satisfaction surveys, after allowing for proper CHAP reserves. CHA's and CHAP's goal will be to reward at least one practitioner in every

category of care-giver in each local board area. CHA boards, in determining the amount of funds available for awards, must wisely balance their duty to reward outstanding professional performance, with their duty to reduce CHAP fees for all members, or at least prevent increases in such fees. One guideline CHA boards may choose to use is that funds for awards must come from professional membership dues not required to be used during the prior year to pay malpractice claim awards. Under this guideline, CHAP health care reserves would not be used to pay awards.

Secondly, the fees obtained from treating Medicare and Medicaid patients will be effectively higher, due to marked reductions in overhead costs paid by professionals and facilities brought about by the efficiencies already discussed. It will be CHAP's responsibility to collect from such third-party payers, and CHAP professionals will be paid approved fees within two weeks just as for services for any CHAP member patients. And, as it becomes clear that CHAP costs are low, smaller numbers of people will be obliged to remain on, or turn to Medicaid programs.

(6) CHA will assist health care professionals in finding out about the most appropriate continuing education programs available, and will endeavor to assure that high quality programs are convenient and affordable.

How Will the Catastrophic Costs of Catastrophic Illness be Managed?

CHA members who wish to enroll in CHAP, and who are already covered by Medicaid and/or Medicare, or other government-paid health care, would continue with such coverage, and would be exempt from paying CHAP fees during such coverage. Similarly, CHA-member patients whose pre-existing policies are paying for current serious or life-threatening illnesses will continue with that coverage, and will also be exempt from CHAP fees during such continued coverage.

CHAP members who fall victim to serious or life-threatening illness after joining CHAP, agree to make reasonable efforts to obtain Medicaid and/or Medicare benefits, if eligible, and if such benefits are forthcoming, such CHAP subscribers will then be excused from paying CHAP fees.

CHA will make every effort to recruit both lay and professional volunteers to mitigate the costs of catastrophic illness among CHAP patients, will place proper emphasis on hospice care rather than hospital care, when appropriate, on avoiding expensive and useless resuscitation attempts on truly terminal patients, and on home care whenever possible without detriment to patient or family. See also the section on "Common Sense" below.

The "right to die with dignity" of terminally ill and irreversibly comatose patients must be respected, as must the right of any patient to refuse treatment while mentally competent. These issues involve human rights, as well as reasonableness and economics. People who want heroic measures taken in circumstances in which expert medical advice unanimously is in agreement that such care is of no benefit to the patient, with a certainty factor approaching 100%, will be required to pay for such care without coverage by CHAP.

In the case of "Acts of God", such as earthquake, flood and hurricane, or in the case of war or civil disturbance, it is to be expected that both government and voluntary organizations such as the Red Cross will continue to give assistance with personnel, materials, money and emergency medical treatment in such extraordinary and disastrous circumstances.

In addition, CHA may from time to time decide to hold special fund-raising events, such as telethons, auctions, 10K runs, marathons, etc., to cover needed funds for costs above subscriber fees collected. Also, CHAP may use some of its collected subscriber fees to buy insurance to cover amounts higher than the total fees collected in a given year.

Responsibility ultimately lies with the community, with all of us, who are the owners of CHA and its CHAP program, to bring into reality all of the economic efficiencies, common sense practices, superior levels of self-care, etc., that will make CHAP work.

Will CHAP Begin With Pilot Programs?

Yes. Professional and lay volunteers will, by their interest and efforts, start the first CHA chapters and begin the first pilot program, or programs, in limited geographic areas or communities. Early success over three or more months beyond a six-month transition phase, or a total of nine months of pilot program operation, is likely to lead to many more local CHA chapters and offerings of CHAP programs. Enrollment into pilot CHAP programs will be based at the offices of participating health care professionals and facilities. During the initial six-month pilot programs, which will be similar to the six-month transition periods in other areas later on, statistical comparisons will be made between CHAP's health outcomes, satisfaction of professionals and patients, and costs — versus results obtained by non-CHAP, concurrently provided services, in the same communities. Toward the end of the fifth month, a decision will be made by each local CHA board whether or not to continue with CHAP on a permanent basis. If the decision is made for a permanent CHAP program, the full transition is to be completed by the end of the sixth month. Malpractice insurance may then be discontinued by the participating professionals and facilities once they have reached the time when they are limiting services exclusively to CHAP members.

Each local CHA board, in launching either a six-month pilot program or a six-month transition program to CHAP, will first require actuarial help to determine the number of members needed to start CHAP, and the initial CHAP fee levels and professional dues levels. Almost inevitably, CHAP pilot programs and initial transition programs will need to include large groups of insureds, and/or large group practices, whether they be HMO's or other types. However, smaller groups of patients and professionals, even individual patients and solo practitioners should also be encouraged to participate in pilot and transitional programs.

How Will the Transition to CHAP Take Place? How Will Members Join? And How Will CHAP Billing Work?

The transition is a six-month period of continuing enrollment and implementation, as is the case for the pilot programs, and it follows a time of several months during which the local CHA board is formed, and health care professionals, facilities and patient groups are recruited. CHA's goal is to have every type of care available in the community, represented as CHAP professional members.

Each participating health professional and facility will inform its patients about CHA and CHAP with literature provided by the local CHA chapters, assisted by regional boards and the national board when these have been organized. Local peer professional and facilities representatives will be chosen to arrange for efficiencies and economies, to establish treatment plan guidelines and approved fee levels. The CHA board must review and approve all treatment plan guidelines and fee schedules, and will monitor and assist all efforts to institute the efficiencies and economies discussed above, such as reduction of duplication of facilities.

All efficiencies are to be in effect or in the advanced stages of being implemented by the CHAP starting date. Some patients will want to continue whatever private health insurance they have during the initial six months, but they will be informed that the participating professionals and facilities plan to limit their practices to CHAP subscribers after the six-month transition period.

Education, publicity, persuasion, the assistance of local and national officials and the news media — all available resources will be utilized to make the recruitment of the community a success. When the public learns about the program and the new reduced fee schedules, enthusiastic enrollment is bound to result. Only the $10 annual CHA membership dues need be paid by those who wish to be actively involved in CHA formation and development. Then, thirty days before CHAP is due to officially begin operation, CHAP fees are due from those joining the program. Those who choose to subscribe to CHAP may pay CHAP fees monthly, quarterly or annually.

CHA's local board will have chosen its CHAP administrator entity prior to the time CHAP fee collection will begin, and all such fees will be forwarded to the administrator. The CHAP administrator will share, with local CHA volunteers, the responsibility for the recruitment of group and individual subscriptions, as well as the recruitment of health care professionals, both individually and as groups, and facilities, all under the authority and with the assistance of the CHA board.

All health care practitioners will be free to cancel their health care malpractice insurance once they are limiting their services to CHAP members (preferably at the end of the six-month transition). Any patient in possession of a CHAP subscriber ID card will have signed the arbitration agreement with CHA.

CHAP subscribers will be free to cancel other health insurance that duplicates CHAP coverage, as of the starting date of their CHAP coverage, except for those patients who have serious or life-threatening conditions covered currently by private insurance. Such patients are required to maintain such insurance, in lieu of paying CHAP fees, for the duration of such serious or life-threatening illness. For such members CHAP benefits will be limited to the benefits provided by the private insurance.

CHAP will be inclusive, and no pre-existing health condition will prevent coverage. However, those members who have Medicare or Medicaid or other governmental forms of health care coverage are to maintain such coverage as long as they are eligible to do so, and during the term of such other coverage, CHAP fees are waived and health care benefits under CHAP are limited to those covered by the governmental benefit program. Those members covered by governmental programs who wish to pay CHAP fees, and are permitted to do so by the appropriate governmental agency, will receive full CHAP benefits.

Patients who present themselves for care after the transition ends, but who have not yet joined CHA or subscribed to CHAP will be able to enroll at the participating health care facility, just as they could have joined during the preceding six months. All health care providers are encouraged to provide urgent, life-saving care to all patients who come, or are brought, to their office or facility, without regard to CHAP coverage, at least until such patients are in stable condition. After stabilization, if the patient or their representatives, such as family, are unable or unwilling to subscribe to CHAP, the patient can be transferred to the care of practitioners and/or facilities who accept non-CHAP subscribers.

Funds will be made available through community fund-raising efforts by CHA to help people subscribe who cannot afford to on their own. An irreducible number of people will never join, even if acts of Congress or state legislatures attempt to mandate membership. Existing laws requiring minimum automobile liability insurance have never succeeded in obtaining full compliance. The goal of CHA activists will be to obtain a minimum of 80% membership in each participating community within two years, and 90% within five years.

Joining CHAP requires reading and signing the CHA membership form which includes the mediation-arbitration agreement, completing a simple CHAP application form, and paying the $10 CHA annual dues plus at least the first month's CHAP subscriber fee. As stated previously, CHAP subscriber fees are likely to fall to about 25% of current health insurance premiums, within two years of CHAP's starting date in any community. The CHAP administrator will propose subscriber fee amounts based on an actuarial study, for CHA's approval. The actuarial study will take into account all of the efficiencies and cost savings that will be in place at inception. Initial fees may be considerably higher than 25% of current health insurance premiums, but even initially, CHA will strive for at least a 25% reduction. Payment will be accepted in cash, check, money order, credit card, or a written promise to pay within thirty days. Each CHAP subscriber will receive a CHAP ID card, similar to a credit card, for the billing to CHAP's administrator of all services rendered. No dollar amount will appear on the voucher, but rather, the type of service rendered and a corresponding numerical code.

CHAP will be a no co-payment system except where decided to the contrary by a two-thirds vote of local or regional boards. No co-payment may ever exceed 5% of the allowable fee for a particular medical service, and inability to pay the co-payment will never result in the service not being provided to the CHAP member/subscriber. Medicaid patients will uniformly be exempt from co-payments regardless of local or regional board co-payment schedules.

People joining CHA without joining CHAP need pay only the $10 annual CHA dues, and the mediation-arbitration agreement need not be signed until they join CHAP as well.

The CHAP administrator will bill the patient's private insurance company or governmental payer, if any, on the patient's behalf, and will credit the account of the providing health care professional or facility with 100% of the agreed CHAP fee within two weeks of having received the CHAP voucher from that health care professional or facility. The CHAP administrator, not health care providers, will wait for the outside third party payment. The member patient, or representative, must sign each voucher for health care, the same as any credit card voucher, and an authorized agent of the health care professional must also sign each voucher. The member is to receive a copy of each voucher, one is to be retained by the provider and the third copy is sent to the CHAP administrator for payment. In some communities, local CHA boards may elect either to permit, or to require, computerized billing. In any case, there will be NO insurance forms except for the patients who have retained private or governmental health insurance as above.

There is never any billing of the member patient or any collecting from the patient for covered CHAP services, unless a co-payment plan, not to exceed 5%, exists as above. However, a CHAP health care professional office or facility may collect, on behalf of CHA and the CHAP administrator, the initial payment by a patient to join CHA and the initial CHAP fee upon joining. Every effort is to be made to set up automatic payment plans for those not paying annually, to help keep both overhead and CHAP fees as low as possible.

The provider's records must document that the services billed to CHAP's administrator were in fact delivered and the need for that service must be documented so that such need will be clearly apparent to any future auditor. Proper medical records would normally suffice.

How Will CHAP Deal With Improper Utilization of Health Care?

Any completely frivolous visits by a CHAP patient member to a CHAP health care provider must be reported to the CHAP administrator together with the billing voucher, and every CHAP member will have signed permission for such reporting as part of the enrollment process. Frivolous demand for health care can lead to CHA restricting all care to a pre-authorization procedure for one year or such other term determined by the local CHA board. Failure by any CHAP health care professional or facility to appropriately report frivolous or unwarranted demands for health care by members can result in disciplinary action against such provider.

Also, all providers will have signed, upon joining CHAP as authorized providers, an agreement that they will promptly report to the CHAP administrator any instance of fraudulent, highly improper or inappropriate, incompetent or negligent care by any CHAP provider, that comes to their attention. The identities of all such reporting professionals will be kept confidential. A similar agreement to report such improper care will be signed by all patient members. Obviously, some subscribers will also be health care professionals, and will therefore have signed reporting provisions in both capacities. Professional peer reviewers will look into claims of impropriety and report their findings to CHA boards for appropriate action as required.

How Will CHAP Interface With Other Health Care Organizations?

CHAP, through its administrators, professional peer representatives, and local CHA boards, will attempt to include HMO's, IPA's and PPO's as CHAP health care professionals and facilities. At the same time, patients who are cared for by these and any other health care providers will be encouraged to join CHAP. It is CHA's intention that it will prove to be necessary for most health care provider organizations to join CHAP in order to keep the loyalty and continuation of their patient populations.

CHA will in effect act as agent for BOTH health care providers and patients, to effectuate the best possible health care plans in each community. Clearly CHA must gain and keep the highest respect as an honest and inclusive broker among all health care professionals and facilities, and among all individual patient members and groups of patient members.

How Will CHAP Help Control the Cost of Medication?

CHAP administrators will buy pharmaceuticals in large quantities at the lowest possible prices from pharmaceutical companies and/or wholesale suppliers for resale via CHAP pharmacists to CHAP members at CHA board-approved prices, and free samples will be solicited from pharmaceutical companies and from physicians and dentists to be pooled for the needy. Local or regional boards may decide to include pharmaceuticals as a covered item under CHAP, which will, of course, accordingly raise the annual fees of local members as compared to CHAP fees where medication costs are not covered.

CHA will work for legislation to be passed requiring pharmaceutical firms operating in the USA to sell in the USA at prices no higher than they charge in other countries for the same quantities of the same product, after allowing a reasonable surcharge for costlier USA regulatory overhead.

What Health Care Services Will Be Covered Under CHAP?

Local boards may include every conceivable form of legally offered health care provided the care offered fits an approved treatment plan by treatment peer groups, as approved by local boards, and provided the care is offered at approved guideline prices.

CHAP administrators in each locale will be available to explain available services and to help members find the care they seek from a CHAP health care professional or facility in the member's area.

Obviously, if pharmaceuticals, dental care, mental health care, and cosmetic surgery and cosmetic dentistry are all included without restriction, except for approved treatment plan and fee guidelines, the CHAP fees in such an area will be considerably higher than in areas providing less inclusive services. It seems likely that most cosmetic surgical procedures that are not related to the treatment of diseases or injuries, will be paid for by patients outside the CHAP system. Each local CHA board will list uncovered health care services that its health care professional members may render by private billing of patients outside of CHAP coverage.

Nationwide uniform standards for CHAP services coverage will probably emerge after the first few years of operation of the system, but some degree of local diversity may persist and should not prove to be a problem. CHAP members traveling to other areas and requiring health care will be eligible for services as though they were in their home region, and billing will be handled by the home region CHAP administrator, per billing procedures using the members' voucher cards.

What Ethical Standards of Practice Will CHAP Professional Members Be Required to Meet?

This difficult subject must be dealt with head on even though there are many thousands of dedicated, fully ethical practitioners in America. But there are also those who practice fraudulently and unethically despite holding proper licenses and credentials. There are dentists who fill non-existent cavities and pull teeth needlessly so that bridgework and dentures can be sold. There are surgeons who perform unnecessary operations, and there are other physicians who order thousands of unnecessary tests, procedures, medications and return visits. There are mental health practitioners who intentionally encourage prolonged courses of therapy primarily based on the patient's ability to pay.

Often there are cases of well-intentioned ordering of expensive tests when a few minutes of truly thoughtful medical history-taking would elucidate the problem. At least a trial of therapy based on opinions drawn from reasonable history-taking and physical examination could be tried in most instances, for some days or a few weeks before resorting to more drastic diagnostic and therapeutic procedures.

In less well-intentioned cases, patients are given injections for no valid medical reason, with the doctor stating that the patient "likes shots". Some Medicaid patients are recycled weekly or bi-weekly for unneeded visits because the system will pay the bills, and the practitioner wants to make up for low Medicaid fees per visit. Also, extra laboratory tests and x-rays will be ordered to beef up the Medicaid billings. Tests will often correspond to the equipment the practitioner happens to own and have in the office, far out of proportion to the real need for the use of such equipment. Some physicians make their patients believe they need bi-weekly B-12 or other injections, or bi-weekly blood pressure exams to monitor non-existent "high" blood pressure for no reason other than to increase the practitioner's income. Prescriptions of potentially dangerous medication are given because some doctors find this easier than spending the time needed to discover the patient's real problem, which may not require any medication. Some physicians justify this practice by saying that if they don't give the patient a prescription, the patient will feel cheated and will change doctors. Some surgeons perform unnecessary surgeries to make up for lower fee schedules imposed by Medicaid, Medicare or other third-party payers.

Under CHAP, the goal is to eliminate ALL of these, and all similar practices. Auditing by CHA peer representatives and CHAP auditors can result in bonus awards for outstanding practitioners as described above, and reprimands, warnings, suspensions and even total ouster from CHAP participation for persistent offenders. Auditing will include interviews with CHAP subscriber/patients and family members when appropriate in order to discover unethical, negligent, incompetent and fraudulent practices. CHAP WILL succeed in massive lowering of the cost of health care, while improving the quality and availability of care!

What Is the Role of Government and Insurance Companies In CHAP?

Government leadership, from the White House to every local level to encourage the development and success of CHAP, would be welcome. Government is an ideal moral sponsor of CHA and CHAP, without needing to be a direct financial or administrative sponsor.

The news media are so closely joined at the hip to whatever government officials say and do that no better publicity and effective backing could possibly be found. On the other hand, grass-roots activists need not wait for any verbal support, from holders of political offices or anyone else, in order to organize local CHA chapters and to get pilot CHAP programs going.

It would be helpful, of course, if government did not attempt to gain control of health care, or interfere with the development of CHAP. Immense relief of budgetary pressures will be afforded by CHAP, which ought to make CHAP very popular with all elected officials. Most importantly, CHA and its CHAP program really can solve the major health care problems in America, through full participation in this system of health care democracy to be established, owned and operated by the community and its activist-volunteers throughout America!

Insurance companies offering health care coverage will continue to do their usual business for a few years, but this will decline as CHAP programs spread. Health insurers may well be able to act as re-insurers of CHAP programs, profiting by protecting CHAP programs against deficits. Some health insurers may wish to become CHAP administrators, and will be permitted to negotiate with CHA chapters for local and regional contracts to administer the system.

What Is the Role of Self-Care in CHAP Programs?

Under the leadership of CHA chapters locally, and with regional and national board support, advances in self-care will become the single greatest cause of improved health, longer lives, fewer injuries and accidents, reduced violence, and of course, avoidance of the whole myriad of preventable illness.

In turn, a key bonus produced by such improved self-care will be a marked reduction in demand for professional health care services, and thus a marked reduction in the cost of health care in America. Prevention of illness and promotion of wellness will pervade community life in our cities and its effects will equally be felt in rural America.

Volunteer CHA members of every local chapter will have rosters of CHA members to call monthly to inquire as to their health and well being. Support groups will help people with all sorts of problems that can lead to illness and injury. Whether it is to help people stop smoking (those who want to) or simply to get a stop sign placed at a dangerous crossing used by school children, CHA's members will be heard!

Volunteers will install smoke alarms in old firetrap hotels, apartments and homes. Neighbors will assist neighbors, community support will be organized, and the spread of homelessness will be reversed. Narcotic addicts will be taught to inhale rather than "shoot up", as was done in the Netherlands, and clean needle exchanges will be provided for those who don't comply. Thus, the spread of AIDS will be reduced! Families under financial and emotional stress will find neighborly help — and professional help when needed — readily available (even before it is asked for under the volunteer monthly call system).

Guideline booklets, cassette tapes, videos and in-person training will be available to help people utilize, and to counsel others in, wellness-promotion, illness and injury prevention, and first aid methods.

Programs to improve self esteem will be run by volunteers under professional guidance (professional volunteers will undoubtedly also participate directly), since self esteem and self-love are necessary forerunners to proper self-care and healthy interpersonal relations.

What Is the Role of Common Sense Medical Care in the Post-Malpractice Insurance Era of CHAP?

Over the past quarter-century, well meaning physicians have been increasingly ordering tests and procedures to protect against possible malpractice suits — tests and procedures that were not really otherwise indicated.

This problem persists, and other serious and costly practices have emerged. As the technology, the range of tests and procedures available have multiplied and the corresponding equipment has become more costly, a growing number of physicians have become motivated, consciously or not, to use their gadgets often to help pay for them, or to make their practices more profitable.

Perhaps more serious is that thousands of physicians have come to believe that high tech tests and procedures are really needed almost all the time. This trend has been concurrent with the trend of physicians cutting down on the time spent taking careful medical histories (making thorough inquiry of each patient as to the history and nature of symptoms, including the circumstances of the patient's personal life that may yield diagnostic clues). Instead, many physicians prescribe high tech tests and procedures, and drugs. One factor operative here is that insurance companies have been paying much better for laboratory tests, x-rays, CAT scans, MRI's, biopsies

234

and other procedures than they do for the time a physician might spend talking to patients to get at the likely real problems so that expensive, and sometimes risky or painful testing and procedures can be rendered unnecessary. Many patients have suffered needless pain, injury and immense expense based on these practices. The time has come to reverse this trend! And Community Health Associations can get the job done.

Patients can participate in the process of restoring common sense to health care by practicing excellent self-care, by exercising common sense in their use of health care professionals, and by questioning tests, procedures and visits that don't seem to make sense to them. Medical "authorities" should be questioned to the point that the patient and/or family understand what the medical situation is and what should be done. Use of independent second opinions is appropriate when doubt remains.

The use of tests and diagnostic procedures as substitutes for proper history-taking and common sense, and the use of "defensive medicine" tactics, are practices that must stop. Peer professional representatives involved in CHAP will establish guidelines for proper evaluation and treatment plans for each category of care giver. Persistent deviation from such plans, without justification, by individual practitioners, could lead to suspension or expulsion by local CHA boards from CHAP participation. Consistent use of such proper guidelines can well lead to financial reward under the CHAP bonus incentive plan described above, especially when exceptionally favorable health outcomes are demonstrated, and/or exceptional patient (and family) satisfaction.

There is no substitute for common sense in medical practice, and today one out of every four or five patients in the hospital is there for the treatment of complications of previous medical treatment and/or testing. The use of a common sense approach in the post-malpractice insurance era will result in immense savings in costs, involvement and suffering. People may be able to regain some confidence in their health and in their own common sense. This includes both physicians and patients. Such a trend reversal could restore all of the benefits of the ART of medical practice, while retaining all of the technological wonders when they are truly

APPENDIX B

needed.

INDEX

INDEX

crime in, 90
Awards, 56, 64, 66, 67, 69, 74, 112,
113, 168, 215, 216, 221, 222,
232

- B -

Baltimore, Maryland
education and, 60, 72
Band-Aid, 3, 13, 40, 41, 48, 109,
182
Barton, Clara, 182
Beck, Carol, 56
Bergdahl, Kay, 60
Berkeley, California, 169
Bickering, 169, 171
Big Brothers, 24, 30, 98, 112
Big Sisters, 30, 98, 112
Bill of Rights, 115
Blacks, 68, 115
Boston University, 72
Boston, Massachusetts, Edison
Project and, 84
Boulder, Colorado, needle
exchanges in, 110
Boys and Girls Clubs, 98, 112, 113
Boys Clubs of New Jersey, 68
Brinkley, Lillian, 60
Britain, drug "harm reduction"
and, 107
Brookings Institution, 57, 67, 83
Brooklyn, New York
civil unrest in, 153
inner-city school in, 56
Bugs Bunny, 68
Bureaucracy, 30, 48, 84, 119, 123,
127, 132, 172
Bush Administration, 65
Business Roundtable, The, 70
Businessmen, education and, 68,
71

- C -

Cain, Paul, 57
California
chartered schools and, 67
drought and, 138
California School Volunteer
Partnership Program, 60
California State University
(Sacramento), internships, 71
Campaigns, 20, 101, 114, 116, 164,
194, 212
Cancer, 98, 99, 101
Capone, Al, 93
Career Academy (Harlem), 66
Carnegie, Andrew, 182
Carter, Jimmy, 11
Center for Educational Innovation
(Harlem), 66
Center on Families, Communities,
Schools & Children's
Learning, 60
Center to Prevent Handgun
Violence, 53
Champus, 214
Channel One, 83
*Charitable Organizations of the
United States*, 26, 172
Chase Manhattan, 68
Chelsea, Massachusetts, schools,
72
Chemical Bank, 68
Chemotherapy, marijuana and, 98,
101
Chernobyl, 130
Chicago, Illinois, 67, 68, 83
Children
abused, 42
and weapons, 30, 53, 55
as teachers, 60
broken homes and, 21

238

INDEX

disadvantaged, 58
Jewish, hidden from
Nazis, 115
marijuana brownies and,
98
Choice
of health care
practitioners, 120,
127, 132, 219, 221
of schools, parental, 18,
61, 62, 65-67, 74, 79,
83, 84-86
Christmas in April, 145
Chubb, John, 57, 67, 83
Churches
as "safe houses", 110
needle exchanges and, 110
Citibank, 68
Clark, Joe, 56
Clean Needles Now (Los
Angeles), 110
Cleaver, Eldridge, 113
Clergy, 13, 18, 51, 73, 115, 144
Clinton Administration, 65, 119
Clinton, Bill, 119
Cocaine, 93, 96, 107, 116, 199
Cold War, 187
College, 55, 56, 58, 67-71, 73, 74,
76, 77, 79-82, 85
Comfort zones, 9
Commitment, 10, 12, 23, 35, 59,
182
Communism, 188
Communitization of schools, 65,
84-86
Community Health Association
(CHA), 20, 119, 120, 132-135,
137, 143, 194, 209-236
Community Health Association
Plan (CHAP), 20, 120, 132,

164, 209-236
Competition among schools, 67,
86
Congress, 101, 115, 119, 133, 197,
227
Congressional aides, 111
Conservative Christians, home
schooling and, 73
Contract-care, impersonal, 127
Coping and drug abuse recovery,
111, 118
Courage, 47, 48, 73, 104, 115, 192
Crime, xiv, xvi, 1-3, 12, 13, 16, 20,
21, 26, 30, 33, 40, 41, 45, 47,
48, 50, 55, 62, 77, 88-90, 92,
96, 97, 98-101, 105, 108, 110,
113, 116, 118, 140, 143, 149,
150, 152, 163, 182, 184, 191,
197, 202, 213
Criminalize(ing), of substance
abuse, 100
Cross, Christopher, 70

- D -
Dade County, Florida, schools, 71
Daniels, John, 109
DeFilippis, Aileen, 66
Democrats, health care solution
of, 127
Department of Education
(California), 64
Department of Justice, 198
Dinkins, Mayor, 109
Disneyland, 58
"Dr. Divorce" and "Dr. Break-Up",
155
Draconian governmental
intervention, 40
Drug cartels, 108
Drug Enforcement Agency

239

(DEA), 104, 198
Drug interactions, 131
Drug Policy Foundation, 98, 99, 116
Drug Wars, 93, 98, 99, 104, 105, 107, 108, 115, 118
see also War on Drugs
Duncan, Joyce, 66
Dutch, illegal drugs and, 107, 108, 110
Dyer, Wayne, 90

- E -

Early Childhood Program (Chelsea, Massachusetts), 72
Eastern Europe, 188
Eastside High School (Paterson, New Jersey), 56
Edison Project, The, 83, 84
Edison, Thomas, xiv
Education Alternatives, Inc., 3, 71, 72
Education First, 69
Educational Excellence for Children with Environmental Limitations (EXXCEL), 58
El Paso, Texas, 57
Electronic Learning System (ELS), 84
Epstein, Joyce, 60
Escalante, Jaime, 56, 63
European countries, illegal drugs and, 107, 108

- F -

Family Development Institute, 58
Family(ies), 5, 87, 93, 97, 98, 114, 174, 182, 198, 234
accomplishments and, 11
America and, 9

broken, 21, 45
counseling, 58
drug abuse and, 116
educational system and, xiv, 76, 77
finances and, 77
health and, 123, 131, 135, 156, 207, 221, 223, 226, 235
law enforcement and, 115
low-income, 86
networking and, 26, 135, 160, 166, 193
"nuclear", 99
problems and, 12, 30, 55
relationships and, 41, 50, 76, 90, 155, 159, 161
responsibility and, 10
thriving, xiv
traditional, 149
tragedies and, 20
Warm Line and, 143-145
Fields, Gerald, 68
Finn, Jr., Chester, 83
First Amendment, 86
First Interstate Bank, 64
Fliegel, Sy, 66
Florida, school violence in, 53
Ford, Betty, 182
French Connection, 105
Frontenac Co., 67

- G -

Galiber, Joseph, 115
Gallup Poll, 2
Garfield High (School, Los Angeles), 63
Genn, Cole, 66
Germans, 188
Gillott, Donald, 71

INDEX

Globe Group, 68
Gobel, George, 32
Golden Apple Foundation, 67
Golle, John, 72
Grass roots, definition of, 10
Gray, James P., 105
Guardian Angels, 30

- H -
Harbor Junior High School for
the Performing Arts,
(Harlem), 65
Harlem's District 4, 65
Harvard University, 69, 80
Hawaii, needle exchanges in, 110
Head Start, 71, 72
Hillel, Jewish scholar, 148
HIV, 109, 110, 126, 130
HMO's, 123, 124, 127, 218, 219,
220, 224, 229
Home and Visiting Teaching,
Mormons and, 155
Home School Legal Defense
Association, The (Falls
Church, VA), 73
Home schooling, 73
Hoover Institution (Stanford
University), 104
Hunter, Dan, 58

- I -
Ichinaga, Nancy, 57
Industrial Areas Foundation, 64
Inglewood, California, 57
Iron Curtain, 187
Irvine Unified School District
(California), 72
Ivy League, 70

- J -
Jeff (author's son), 99
Jewish children, hiding of from
Nazis, 115
Johns Hopkins University, 60
Jones, Allen, 66
Junior (community) colleges, 79,
80
Junior High School 117 (Harlem),
65

- K -
Kansas City, 68
Kaplan, Edward, 109
Kauffman, Ewing Marion, 68
Kellman, Joe, 68
Kelly, Walt, 171
Kentucky, school officials in, 63
King, Jr., Martin Luther, xiv, 172,
182
Koch (Charles G.) Foundation, 68
Koch, Mayor, 109
Koldyke, Martin "Mike", 67
Kopp, Wendy, 70

- L -
Latin America, 130, 187
Lean on Me, 56
Lightner, Candy, 131
Links, Inc., 69
Long Beach, California, 60
Loreto, Thomas, 90
Los Angeles, 23, 58, 64, 99
needle exchanges in, 110
riots, 16, 153
Los Angeles Educational Alliance
for Restructuring Now
(LEARN), 64
Los Angeles Educational
Partnership (LAEP), 64

241

Los Angeles Unified School
District, 61, 64
Louis Harris (poll), 64
Lowell, Massachusetts, Edison
Project and, 84

- M -
Magnet schools, 58
Managed competition, 127
Manhattan Institute, 66
Marion Laboratories, 68
Mariotti, Steve, 68
Maryland, school program in, 60
Massachusetts Department of
Education, 84
Massachusetts Institute of
Technology (MIT), 57
McDermott, Mimi, 66
Meals on Wheels, 16, 30
Medicaid, 48, 123, 124, 214, 222,
226, 227, 231, 232
Medicare, 48, 120, 123, 124, 214,
222, 226, 232
Miami, Florida
civil unrest in, 153
crime in, 90
school contracting by, 71
Middle schools, 64
Minneapolis, school contracting
by, 72
Minnesota, charter schools and,
66, 67
Moe, Terry, 57, 67
Monroe, Lorraine, 66
Moore, Cosetta, 69
Moore, Leslie, 66
Morris, Rick, 62
Mothers Against Drunk Driving
(MADD), 131

- N -
Nader, Ralph, 182
National Association of
Elementary School Principals,
60
National Association of Partners
in Education, 61
National Association of Secondary
School Principals, 56
*National Directory of Non-Profit
Organizations*, 26, 172
National Foundation for Teaching
Entrepreneurship (NFTE), 68
Nazis, 115
NCAA, 80
Needle exchanges, 109, 110
Neighborhood Environmental
Committee, 145
Neo-Nazi violence, 188
Netherlands, illegal drugs in, 107
New American Schools
Development Corp., 65
New Haven, Connecticut, needle
exchanges in, 109
New York
education, 66, 68
needle exchanges in, 109,
110
Next Century Schools (program),
70
Nichols, Duane, 56
9-1-1, 20, 131, 143
Nobel Prize, 130
Notre Dame, 11

- O -
Olmos, Edward James, 15
Oregon, home schoolers and, 73

INDEX

SEE REVERSE SIDE OF THIS PAGE FOR ORDER FORM

BOOK ORDER FORM
(YOU MAY PHOTOCOPY THIS PAGE)

Telephone Orders: Call Toll Free (800) 333-5867. Please have your VISA or MasterCard ready.

Fax Orders: (417) 336-2487

Mail Orders:
Send to: Grass-Roots Press
P.O. Box 7609
Branson, Missouri 65615-7609

Please send me _____ copies of "*JUMP-STARTING AMERICA: The Grass-Roots Revolution.*" I understand that I may return any books for a full refund — for any reason, no questions asked.

Please send my book(s) to:

Name:_____
Organization
or Company Name (if any):_____
Address:_____
City:_____ **State:**_____ **Zip:** _____

NO CHARGE FOR SHIPPING!! JUST SEND $17.95 U.S.A. OR $23.50 CANADIAN FOR EACH BOOK ORDERED. Please add 7.225% sales tax for books to be mailed to Missouri addresses.

Payment (check one):
□ **My check is enclosed**
□ **Bill my VISA card number:**_____
□ **Bill my MasterCard card number:**_____

IF CREDIT CARD TO BE BILLED:
PLEASE GIVE NAME ON CARD:_____
AND PLEASE GIVE EXPIRATION DATE ON CARD:_____

YOU CAN ORDER TOLL FREE 24-HOURS A DAY by calling:
(800) 333-5867

You may want to consider "*JUMP-STARTING AMERICA: The Grass-Roots Revolution*" as a gift book for family and friends.